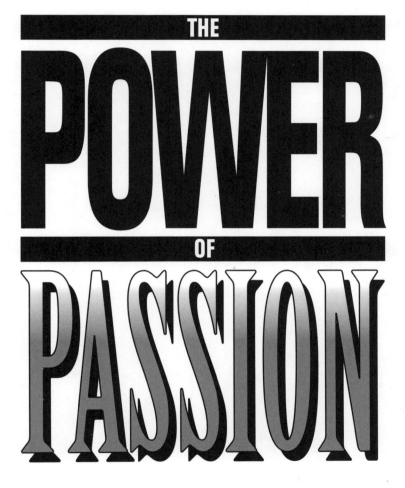

THE POWER OF PASSION

THE POWER OF PASSION

OF

ACHIEVE YOUR OWN EVERESTS

ALAN HOBSON AND JAMIE CLARKE
PROFESSIONAL SPEAKERS & EVEREST SUMMITEERS

Canadian Cataloguing in Publication Data

Hobson, Alan, 1958 -
        The power of passion

ISBN 0-9682430-0-2

        1. Motivation (Psychology). 2. Mountaineering—Everest, Mount (China and Tibet)—Psychological aspects. I. Clarke, Jamie, 1968- II. Title.

BF505,G6H62 1997   I58.1   C97-901095-0

Edited by Leslie Johnson
Design: VBG, Santa Clara, CA
            David Advertising, Calgary, AB
            Stewart Publishing, Calgary, AB
Photographs: Front Cover — Jamie Clarke
            Back Cover — Bruce Kirkby

Printed in Canada

The Power of Passion

Dedication

To all the Canadians who have climbed on Everest before us, whose raw courage and determination have been an inspiration, and whose commitment and tenacity we have tried in some small way to emulate. They are, and will always remain, our mentors and heroes. Nothing we have done, nor will ever do, would be possible without them. They have helped guide our lives. Of special meaning to us are:

John Amatt	John McIsaac
Rusty Baillie	Pat Morrow
Mario Bilodeau	James Nelson
Barry Blanchard	Bruce Patterson
James Blench	Tim Rippel
Denis Brown	Laurie Skreslet
Dwayne Congdon	Albi Sole
Kevin Doyle	Peter Spear
Lloyd "Kiwi" Gallagher	Hank Van Weelden
Dan Griffith	Sharon Wood
Bill March	

The Power of Passion

Contents

Acknowledgments   v

Introduction: Everyday Everests   ix

Opening: Before We Get to Base Camp   xi

Chapter 1: Daring to Dream   1

Chapter 2: Finding a Friend   7

Chapter 3: Preparing to Climb   19

Chapter 4: The Must of Trust   25

Chapter 5: Overcoming Our Fear of Heights   35

Chapter 6: The Triumph in a Team   45

Chapter 7: Victory Through Effort   59

Chapter 8: Re-Engineering the Dream   71

Chapter 9: Choosing a High Performance Team   89

Chapter 10: Facing Death   97

Chapter 11: Communication Breakdown   109

Chapter 12: Rising to the Challenge of Change   123

Chapter 13: The Power of Love   139

Chapter 14: Choosing People Over Peaks   153

Chapter 15: Refusing to Fold   171

They Did It!   187

About the Authors   189

There's More Where This Came From   191

Acknowledgments

— ALAN —

This book was a team effort. As Jamie and I ramped up toward departure for our third expedition to Everest, it was a challenge to get this book done before leaving for Asia. We could not have done it alone.

We are greatly indebted to:

Mary Ross, of The Everest Effort Inc., our speaking company, whose patience and assistance in acting as an intermediary between book sources, transcription and proofreading services, couriers and ourselves was invaluable. She is a cheerful woman who retains her equanimity even under pressure.

Karen Harris, our Marketing Director at The Everest Effort Inc., who not only designed our travel schedules for speaking presentations with the book and physical training in mind, but who also helped keep us financially solvent while we worked on this and other projects simultaneously. She has tremendous energy.

Sandy Pearson, of The Odyssey Adventure Society, the expedition arm of our operation, for the hours she spent transcribing Jamie's contributions. She also worked incredibly hard taking a load off Jamie so he might have time to help write this book as well as organize the Colliers/Lotus Notes Everest Expedition. She genuinely cares about others.

Cathy Moore and Darlene Cook of Cameleen Transcription Services and Nadyne Shafe of Calgary Business Services, whose swift and accurate transcription and proofreading was essential in making this book a reality.

Gina Comeau, of the Westin Harbour Castle Hotel in Toronto, Canada, who worked until 12:45 a.m. one morning transcribing a two-hour telephone interview with John McIsaac so I might take it with me on a flight the next day. Her professionalism and poise into the wee small hours was impressive. She never once complained.

Leslie Johnson, who edited the book and acted as production coordinator for the project. Leslie is the finest editor with whom we have worked. She is not only a skilled text editor, but her substantial creative experience in broadcasting and magazine writing enabled her to make creative suggestions that substantially improved the quality of the manuscript. She is also an experienced mountaineer and a fine friend.

Denis Brown, John McIsaac, Tim Rippel and Mario Bilodeau, members of both the '91 and '94 Everest expeditions. Without them, we would have far less of a story. Their contributions not only to the expeditions, but to this book helped produce what we believe is a powerful product. They are men of great courage and conviction. They belong on Everest.

— JAMIE —

For years, I have been a student in the mountains and for the last seven years Everest has been my most influential teacher. On Everest in 1991, I earned an undergraduate degree. As the co-organizer and primary leader of the 1994 Emergo Mt. Everest Expedition, I completed my Masters work. Now, I look forward to making some progress on my doctorate on Everest in 1997.

Some of what I have learned rests in these pages. It was a gift to me made possible by the unconditional support of numerous friends and colleagues. None of what I have experienced and learned would have been possible without the continuous encouragement of my family. Of special note are...

My brother, Leigh, my first hero. His early travels to far off places inspired me to adventure. None of my subsequent adventures would have happened if not for his endless contributions. He is not only my brother — he is one of my best friends.

My father, Ian Clarke, who continues to teach me, and with whose honesty we build our friendship.

What strength and courage I have I owe to my mother, Denise Keller.

For Janet McMahen's prodding questions, insights and friendship, I thank her.

For her selflessness, I thank Karen Vail, who encouraged me to go to Everest in 1991 knowing it would, in part, cost us our relationship.

Then, there is the woman I love, Barbara Neumann, who entered my mountain world and broke down the emotional walls I once hid behind. Her love, patience and understanding amid my self-centered pursuits have taught me the meaning of compassion.

The Power of Passion

Introduction:
Everyday Everests

In one way or another, we are all mountaineers climbing our own mountains. Some of us are climbing marriage mountains, parenting mountains and professional mountains. Others are climbing health mountains, financial mountains, debt mountains and relationship mountains. Regardless of who we are or where we live, there is one thing we all share. We share struggle — the struggle to succeed, to better ourselves, or to create a better life for our families and loved ones. Some days, it's a struggle to get out of bed.

Life's "Everyday Everests" are just as real as Everest itself. Jamie and I believe they are harder to surmount than Everest because they are longer-term. An Everest expedition lasts about two months. We prepare; we go there; we climb. If we're fortunate, we make it to the top and return safely. Life goes on.

Our "Everyday Everests" aren't like that. There are no definite "summits." No one takes our picture or congratulates us when we get to the summit because there is no summit.

The everyday mountains we climb keep getting higher. The loads we carry up them are becoming heavier, and our environment is changing almost as fast as mountain weather. The metaphorical crevasses, avalanche slopes, high winds, and cold keep coming at us.

In this book, Jamie and I want to share with you the story of our struggle to climb Everest. It's a story of hopes and dreams, of tragedy and tenacity. Mostly, it's a story about triumph — a triumph of the human spirit. Through our friendship, Jamie and I have learned the power of passion. We have learned how two very different people can achieve new heights if they share a common goal and a burning desire to work towards it, no matter what the obstacles.

We hope our story helps you climb your own Everests.

Before We Get to Base Camp

"(There is more than) one true account of an expedition. There are as many versions of the truth as there are participants."

— Reinhold Messner, world's greatest living mountaineer, *Expedition to the Ultimate*, London: New York: Kaye @ Ward, Oxford University Press, 1979.

The Power of Passion

Daring to Dream 1

– ALAN –

In our all-out attempt to save John's life, we had forgotten about Denis. Denis had also made an attempt on the world's tallest peak without bottled oxygen and he had been up all night tending to his patient. He hadn't slept for at least four nights. Denis was also exhausted. A moment later, we found out how exhausted he was. At the top of the north ridge, at 25,000 feet, not more than 10 feet from me, Denis Brown fell.

I can still see him clearly now. He's sliding down the snow on his stomach, spinning wildly out of control. His ice ax flies out of one hand. His camera flies out of the other. I hear him cry out, but there's nothing I can do.

It's obvious what's going to happen. He's going to continue spinning, he's going to go over the edge, and he's going to fall 4,000 feet to the Main Rongbuk Glacier.

Denis Brown is going to die and there's nothing I can do but watch him fall.

It was like some kind of crazy, slow motion horror show. For some reason, I felt almost disconnected from the scene. I didn't feel any fear. I just defaulted to reporter mode. I picked up my radio and said:

"Denis has fallen. Stand by for more information."

*   *   *

It was at moments like these that I found myself asking the inevitable question: Why? Why climb Everest? Why assume such risk — and not just assume it, but volunteer for it? Prepare for it? Train for it?

The answer to the question "why" goes far deeper than the oft-quoted phrase, "Because it's there." To understand why some human beings are driven to choose challenge and risk, we need to return to something basic to all of us on this planet. We need to return to dreams.

My dream began the way so many dreams do, in a rather obscure place and in a seemingly ordinary way. There was no fanfare. In fact, there was no indication whatsoever that anything special was going to take place at all.

Since I'd been a boy, I'd dreamed of going to Mount Everest. Even before I could read, I knew what Mount Everest looked like. I'd seen pictures of it in books. I was drawn to it. I don't know why. Nothing in my family upbringing or background said I should be. I just was.

When I learned to read, I became fascinated with stories about the mountain. It wasn't just that it was the world's tallest peak. It was the human drama the mountain produced. "What was there about this particular mountain," I asked myself, "that made men and women do these amazing things?" Over and over in accounts I read, there were examples of human beings doing things they weren't supposed to be able to do — such as survive at high altitude for days when scientists said they could only survive a few hours. Or, climbers endured horrendous conditions in extreme cold and howling winds when experts said they would perish.

What captured me was not the mountain itself. It was

what the mountain did to men and women. Everest seemed to have a presence, a power — the ability to transform the ordinary into the extraordinary. I wanted to find out for myself what that power was.

Everest seemed to have a presence, a power — the ability to transform the ordinary into the extraordinary.

In 1989, when I learned there was a Canadian expedition going to Everest, I phoned the expedition leader.

"You don't know me," I said brashly to Peter Austen, then in Prince George, British Columbia, a lumber town about 500 miles northeast of Vancouver, "but you can't go to Mount Everest without me."

I'm sure Peter was less than impressed. Although I had rock and ice climbing experience, I had no high altitude climbing experience, no money and no connections to potential sponsors.

"What do you mean?" he said assuredly. "I already am. We've got a permit, and we're going in the fall of 1991 — with or without you."

I swallowed hard and buoyed up my courage.

"Do you have sponsors for your climb?" I inquired.

"Yes, of course," he said, his voice telegraphing irritation.

"Could you tell me why those sponsors are involved in your expedition?"

"Well, for many reasons, some of which include publicity, promotion, and exposure."

"And how will your climb give them that?"

"Well, that's up to the sponsors."

"What do you mean?"

"Our job is to climb the mountain," Peter said. "Their job is to capitalize on the opportunities the event creates."

I saw my chance.

"How will people back home know about the event?" I asked.

"Through media coverage, of course."

"So you're bringing reporters to the mountain?"

"No, I wouldn't dream of it."

"Then how will the media get news about your expedition?"

There was a pause at the other end of the line. I hoped I had caught his interest.

The 1991 "Climb for Hope" — the first Everest expedition staged to raise awareness of a charity — had no way to get news back to North America except by mail. Without a communications link, Peter could not get media coverage for his expedition, or for its charity, Rett Syndrome, a neurological disorder that afflicts infant girls. Without media coverage, I believed Peter could not give the expedition's sponsors the profile they wanted.

The expedition needed a live satellite telephone uplink from the mountain. I hoped to provide it. After weeks of persistent calling, Peter eventually agreed to meet with me.

It is more important to have a dream than to have a way to achieve it. If the power of our passion is strong enough, we will figure out a way to make our dreams reality.

After I explained how such a communications system could work, he reluctantly agreed to let me join the expedition. I could join the team not so much as a climber, although he did agree to let me climb, but as a freelance writer, journalist, and broadcaster. I'd made my living doing that for about eight years.

To understand the power of my passion for Everest, you need to know that when I approached Peter, I not only had no high altitude climbing experience, I had no satellite telecommunications experience. I also had no money to rent a $250,000 system either. Nor did I have an office or staff. All I had was my small, two-bedroom apartment in Calgary, Canada. In short, I had nothing except a dream — and a large amount of naiveté.

A dream can be a powerful thing. It is more important to have a dream than to have a way to achieve it. If the power of our passion is strong enough, we will figure out a way to make our dreams reality. It is more than having the will to find the way. Will is a conscious act. Passion is deeper. It involves emotion and intuition. If passion is properly tapped, it creates tremendous drive.

I was driven by what I saw as an exciting opportunity. Canadians had never sent satellite telephone reports from Everest. I wanted to hear the words, "From Mount Everest, this is Alan Hobson reporting," more than anything. I thought it would be exciting. It was more important to me than climbing the mountain. That would come later. First, I wanted to see if I could get reports off Everest.

The Power of Passion

Finding a Friend 2

For two years, it looked like I might not pull off my communications dream. Because I had no telecommunications experience, my learning curve was steep. Every phone call I made brought more questions. Every question I asked led to a higher financial need. Without an emergency injection of money from my parents, who are far from wealthy, I would never have survived financially. It was hard just to pay the rent, let alone put together a telecommunications system to be used halfway around the world on the side of the world's tallest peak.

The expedition had no money to lend me. Its budget was already stretched to the limit staging the climb. As I struggled to pay the bills, I also struggled to keep my communications dream alive.

After two years, it became obvious I couldn't do it alone. The expedition was three months away, I was almost broke, and I still needed money. The good news? I had located a portable satellite dish and a sponsor to underwrite its rental. The bad news? I couldn't afford to ship the system to the mountain. I was $5,000 short.

Five thousand dollars may not seem like a lot to some people, but at the time, it represented about a third of my annual income. I felt like I was standing at the edge of a crevasse — I knew where I had to go, I just had no way to bridge the gap — at least not yet. Even if I somehow came up with the money, I still needed someone to help me operate the system on Everest.

Enter Jamie Clarke. We'd met in 1987 when I'd been asked by a local magazine to write a story about Calgarians who might compete in the 1988 Olympic Winter Games in Calgary. He was a three-time Canadian junior cross-country ski champion.

I'll never forget the first time I spoke to Jamie. Like the first one I had with Peter Austen, it was another important telephone conversation, and in retrospect, probably one of the most significant of my life.

"So Jamie, what are you doing for training?" I asked.

"Well, I'm doing endurance and sprint training."

"Sprint training, huh. Where do you do sprint training?"

"In Fish Creek Park."

Fish Creek Park is a hilly, wooded provincial park in Calgary. It has no running track, let alone any straight, flat areas, except perhaps the odd bicycle path. Besides, it is full of stumps, deadfall, gopher holes, underbrush and animals. You don't do sprint training in Fish Creek Park.

> *I'll never forget the first time I spoke to Jamie…it was another important telephone conversation, and in retrospect, probably one of the most significant of my life.*

"What exactly do you do for sprint training in Fish Creek Park?" I asked.

There was a pause.

"Well," Jamie finally said… "I chase deer."

"You and I have to get together," I said.

That was it. My life changed

from that moment, Jamie would become one of my most trusted friends. He was singularly driven, but fun; intense, yet easy-going. He was special.

– JAMIE –

My friendship with Alan really began when he invited me home for dinner. There, I met Theresa, then Alan's wife, a student at the University of Calgary. They were just 28, yet they seemed much older than I was.

Theresa was kind, soft-spoken, and attractive. She patiently listened to Alan and me as we shared stories of our past athletic pursuits. Oddly, Everest was not mentioned that night, nor was mountain climbing of any kind.

When I left their house, I had no inclination my life had taken a turn. Over time, however, as is the case with any subtle navigational correction, my course and destination changed dramatically.

— ALAN —

The moment I met Jamie, I sensed we were kindred spirits, although we have very different personal styles. He was 18 then. I was born and raised in Canada, I had also been a national-level gymnast in the United States and had worked as a freelance journalist overseas. We formed a potent team.

While I am an intense, strategic, and detail-oriented thinker, Jamie is spontaneous and creative. I am single-minded and happiest when I am focused on one thing I love to do. Jamie thrives on variety and is loved by many people. Although he delights in his own solitude, particularly in the mountains, he is intense in his relationships with others. We complement each other beautifully.

Jamie was the only guy I knew who was fit enough and keen enough to join me on my Everest training sessions. He has an amazing ability to make even the most mundane tasks, like climbing stairs with a heavy pack, enjoyable. He has a wonderful sense of humor, a razor-sharp wit and an even sharper intellect. He is also a man of solid integrity and balanced values. You can count on him, especially in a crisis.

When I mentioned one day that I might need a person to assist me with the communications system on Everest, I opened the floodgates on an outpouring of enthusiasm and energy from Jamie. I would return to my apartment and find my answering machine filled with telephone messages from him proclaiming his desire to join me on the mountain.

"I'll do whatever it takes," he said in one of his messages. "I'll sell my car, borrow from my grandparents, work two jobs, whatever. If you need me, I'm there."

Eventually, as time ticked by to departure, Jamie's enthusiasm won me over. Together, we struck a deal — he agreed to help get the communications system to the mountain if I covered expenses and lobbied to get him on the team.

As I discovered, Jamie and I shared more than a fascination with Everest. Like me, he was also a passionate adventurer.

— JAMIE —

My first recollection of life came with the rhythm of a dogsled, bundled up in a sleeping bag and being pulled along behind the powerful legs of Nanook, our family's malamute. There, between naps, I watched the countless peaks of the Canadian Rockies float by, only to be jettisoned suddenly from the warmth of my cocoon when the sled tipped over on a sharp corner and my face smashed into the snow. Nanook was never conscious of her cargo. Frozen steaks, or small children, were pulled alike.

My parents divorced when I was three and my mother, Denise, married Michael Keller. My mother has been a constant source of love and inspiration. I owe my successes to her. She is an angel.

Michael introduced me to the mountains where now, 25 years later, I find my most basic peace. Mike treated me with the care and love he would have given his own son.

> *Amidst the wind and cold, rock and snow, danger and beauty, I uncover truth, and I find meaning and peace.*

Although I had regular contact with my natural father, I struggled to develop my relationship with him, separated as we were. Yet I have never doubted the intensity of his love for me. Caught between two families, I was confused. With Michael, I sometimes found the father/son relationship I needed and wanted, but although he was always helpful and interested in me, the quality of our relationship was not consistent. I think this had more to do with me than it did with him. I wanted a father's guidance — to have one constant dad.

In the mountains, I found what I was missing: counsel, answers, encouragement and strength. The mountains have helped me realize all of this is within me. The mountains became, in part, the father I needed. Yet they are a mute parent, forcing me to listen to my own thoughts. The cold rocks cannot offer the wisdom of past experience like a father can. Today, my Dad and I are making up time we lost earlier in our lives. I still go to the mountains seeking self-knowledge. Amidst the wind and cold, rock and snow, danger and beauty, I uncover truth, and I find meaning and peace.

We are, I think, the culmination of our experience and ancestry. They propel us onto the stage of life where we grow and ultimately perform, and where we may or may not choose to engage in trying to answer the more profound questions of our spiritual essence.

I am half French Canadian, as well as a mix of Scottish and English. Both my grandfathers endured difficult, but vastly different times in the '30s. They served during the Second World War, one as a sailor in the Royal Canadian Navy, the other as a fighter pilot in the RCAF. One came from rural Alberta, where I spent some of my early years; the other came from a prominent colonial family in Barbados. I have awe and respect for both of them.

This widely cosmopolitan group of ancestors has given me a wide view of the world. My brother and I traveled to east Africa when we were in our early 20s and during that time, it was wonderful to lay over with distant but friendly relatives in the Kenyan highlands. Making journeys into other cultures is a natural part of my background and this has made my distant adventures times of learning and wonderment, rather than times of bewilderment or trepidation.

My spiritual journey has also been diverse. My ethos is an eclectic collection of traditional Christian churches. My natural father is the black sheep of the family, having found his sense of meaning in evangelical Christianity. I still seek to comprehend all of my religious background, while maintaining contact with a wide variety of other faiths.

> *The mountains have become my theater for spiritual self-exploration. The mountains and my adventures in them have become the bright light I use to illuminate my innermost self.*

The mountains have become my theater for spiritual self-exploration. The mountains and my adventures in them have become the bright light I use to illuminate my innermost self. It is here that I find my truth. It is here that I learn to face the raw reality of who I am. This is why I climb and adventure and will continue to for many more years.

— ALAN —

My childhood was different from Jamie's. I grew up in Ottawa, Canada, about 500 miles north of New York City. My father, Dr. John Peter Hobson, was a vacuum physicist with the National Research Council. He spent 32 years doing leading edge scientific research. My mother, Isabel Margaret, a top

The outcome of that I.Q. test drove deep into my psyche and to some extent, still affects my behavior today. It has helped produce a driven, high-achiever who will only accept perfection — a very unhealthy way to live.

graduate in physical education at McGill University in Montreal, was a full-time mother and homemaker for me and my three brothers before she turned to work outside the home later in life.

My childhood went along normally until one day in elementary school. At that time, the grading system was basic: 1 was Excellent; 2 was Very Good, 3 was Good, 4 was Poor and 5 was Unsatisfactory. I had been fortunate enough to receive all 1s in my subjects except for one 2. It was considered necessary for me to take an I.Q. test to determine what "stream" I should go into the next year.

I did poorly on the I.Q. test. I remember how frustrated I became when I was unable to manipulate colored blocks to duplicate the pattern given to me on the test paper in the time allotted. But I never gave up. The examiner had to physically remove the blocks from my hands to get me to move to the next part of the test.

I came away from that hour-long exam feeling disillusioned. It had not measured my determination or commitment, I thought, nor had anyone ever given me a blank sheet of paper and said, "Here. Write us a story." Thus, they had no measure of my creative ability either.

The next year, most of my friends, who apparently had done better on the I.Q. test than I had, went into the "accelerated" stream. One of my classmates, who had had all 1s in her subjects, had not been required to take the I.Q. test at all. She had instantly been accelerated. Meanwhile, I stayed back with the rest of the "normal" students. The way I saw it, if my friends were "accelerated," that meant I was slower. That made me angry.

From that day forward, I vowed that never again would any system of any kind ever limit me, especially academically. I committed myself not just to getting great grades, but to getting perfect grades all the way through the rest of elementary school, high school and university. Nothing below an "A" would be tolerated because that way no one could accuse me of being slower. The outcome of that I.Q. test drove deep into my psyche and to some extent, still affects my behavior today. It has helped produce a driven, high-achiever who will only accept perfection — a very unhealthy way to live.

I do not blame the educational system for what happened. I was too young to know what was happening. I only know how I chose to react.

My mother insisted the I.Q. test was meaningless — that the school didn't use it for anything. But that's not how I saw it, nor still see it now. I saw that the system had discounted my effort and grades and judged me only on the basis of a silly test. It made me determined to prove them wrong.

While life at school had its challenges, my home life was very stable. My parents were always supportive of me. They gave me many gifts, including lots of time, particularly as a boy; unconditional love, positive role models, good values, and something I call "limitless thinking." I was never told, for example, that I was physically or mentally

I came to believe that even something as outlandish as Everest was possible.

incapable of doing anything. And, I was never told I was stupid, or lazy — something I heard my friends' parents say to them. Thus, I came to believe that even something as outlandish as Everest was possible.

I think that letting your child do something potentially life-threatening is the ultimate demonstration of love. Although my parents, like Jamie's, have had difficulty with my adventuring, they have accepted it as part of who I am and have loved me unconditionally. I know I have caused them many sleepless nights. Although I'm sure they'd prefer I didn't take risks, I know they don't care if I climb Mount Everest or sell stamps. All they care about is whether I'm happy. Like Jamie, I have been blessed with wonderful parents.

So, there Jamie and I were, just a couple of penniless guys with a big dream. As it turned out, that was enough to get started. As Carl Sandburg, the American poet and biographer, said, "Nothing happens unless first a dream." We definitely had that — and we had each other for support.

— JAMIE —

Alan stands a little over five feet, five inches tall, but his physical strength and intensity of character add considerable height. His years of training in gymnastics gyms have left him rippled with muscle that I've always appreciated. Today, having not competed in over 15 years, he still looks the part and is able to execute many of the stunts he once used as part of his arsenal in gymnastics competitions. I wish I could have seen him perform then. It would have been a display of athletic artistry.

Alan has the strength of character to accomplish great things. I've always thought that about him. I can count on him to show up not only on game day, but to all the practices as well. And he will keep playing well after the sun has set and everyone else has gone home. In many ways, this has been the key to our success. We simply keep playing in the darkness. In those dark times, Alan and I became friends.

— ALAN —

Everest was something I desperately needed at that time in my life. A few years earlier, my marriage of four and a half years to Theresa had ended, leaving me lonely and emotionally devastated. To date, surviving and growing from my divorce ranks as the most difficult thing I have ever done. It was far more difficult than Everest. It took far longer to overcome, hurt far more and in a way much deeper than Everest. It was like my soul was at war with itself. My self-esteem, self-concept, and sense of self-worth were badly shaken and it took years until I felt emotionally stable again. During that difficult grieving and re-building period, I carried the pain of my divorce with me, and to some extent I

> *Alan has the strength of character to accomplish great things. I can count on him to show up not only on game day, but to all the practices as well. He will keep playing well after the sun has set and everyone else has gone home.*

always will. It was like a tearing of my emotional insides. Theresa was wonderful to me, but I put too much emphasis on my career, and my ambition cost me my marriage. "Love conquers all things save one —," I remember reading at the time — "neglect." I neglected Theresa and it cost me dearly. If she were here, I would

Surviving and growing from my divorce ranks as the most difficult thing I have ever done. It was far more difficult than Everest.

apologize to her and tell her how special she is, but I have not seen her since we split up. She re-married shortly after our divorce and while it has always been my goal to re-marry, it has not yet come to pass. Learning to trust again has been a major mountain for me to climb.

— JAMIE —

Everest was part of the answer to Alan's divorce. It gave him a goal, a focal point on which to focus his energies. I needed a new mountain to climb too. At 15, I had stood on the podium to accept a gold medal as Canadian junior cross-country ski champion, but inexplicably, I felt little more than emptiness.

The focus of my training had been to be Number One, to stand on top. But when I actually stood there and received all the accolades, I wasn't as happy as I thought I would be. I was missing something. To discover what was missing took a few more years of racing and a journey to Everest.

After the junior championship, I dedicated myself to representing Canada in cross-country skiing at the 1988 Olympic Winter Games in Calgary. My Olympic dream failed to materialize. Just before the Winter Games came to my home town, I fell sick with mononucleosis, a viral disease that affects the white blood cells. The patient becomes drained of energy. My Olympic dream had already evaporated. I had failed to ski even close to Olympic standards. I was more ambitious than able. This realization had a profound effect on me. I was physically and emotionally crushed.

— ALAN —

Jamie and I shared a sense of personal disillusionment. After 10 years as a competitive gymnast, I too had experienced a disappointment. I finished second at the U.S. National Gymnastics Championships, missing the gold medal by five one-hundredths of a point. When the results were announced, I went behind the stands and wept. The song that played on the public address system that day remains ingrained in my memory. It was Supertramp's *Take the Long Way Home*. I did — 900 miles by bus back to my parents and family in Ottawa when my university education was completed a few months later.

To understand how two so otherwise successful athletic careers had culminated with each athlete feeling he had failed, you need look no further than the sports pages. Like many North American kids, Jamie and I had been raised on the adage made famous by the football coach, Vince Lombardi. He said: "Winning isn't everything — it's the only thing."

After our athletic careers ended, Jamie and I needed to feel a sense of challenge and accomplishment again. We knew we would never be able to change our pasts. What we needed was a new future. For so many years, high performance sport had been an integral part of our lives.

Soon, we were about to experience high performance of a different sort.

Preparing to Climb 3

Those last three months before leaving for Everest in 1991 were amongst the most frantic of our lives. We pulled out all the stops, working and training 16 hours a day.

Every day, after we had finished being rejected on the telephone by potential sponsors of our communications system, we loaded our backpacks with up to 85 pounds. I used copies of my bestseller, *Share the Flame*, which gave an account of the 1988 Olympic Torch Relay. Jamie filled his pack with bags of water and outdoor equipment. Together, we hauled ourselves into the stairwell of a downtown Calgary office tower.

Finding a stairwell wasn't a challenge. Getting permission to climb the stairs was a challenge. Most of the building managers were concerned about liability.

"What if you fall, injure yourselves and sue us?" they asked.

Time for a solution. My brother, Eric, was president of a successful oil and gas marketing firm downtown. He asked his building manager for help and within 24 hours, Jamie and I had the permission we needed.

The north tower of the SunLife Plaza in Calgary became

our mountain of concrete and rebar. It had, appropriately enough, 29 floors. Since Everest was 29,028 feet high, perhaps it was a coincidence — if you believe in coincidence. For about three hours at a time, we climbed those grueling 29 stories, visualizing ourselves climbing Everest. When we reached the roof, we took the elevator down to ground. Then we'd repeat the process until we'd done about eight to 10 circuits (about 290 stories, or about 3,000 vertical feet).

Those thousands of steps in that stairwell helped make our Everest dream reality. Eddie Cantor, an American entertainer, perhaps described the success process best when he said: "It takes 20 years to become an overnight success."

A friend of ours, Vince Poscente, who competed in the sport of speed skiing at the 1992 Olympic Winter Games in Albertville, France, has a theory on success he calls his "Dye in the Bucket Principle." Now a successful professional speaker living in Dallas, Texas, Vince went from being a recreational skier to competing in the Olympic final in just five "short" years.

Vince likens the dream-building and preparation process to dropping a single drop of red dye into a bucket of water every day. At first, it doesn't look like anything's happening — the water appears completely clear. Then, after a few weeks, a hint of pink appears. After months, this hue becomes clearly pink, then months later, light red and then dark red. Eventually, we can't even see through the water that was once completely clear.

Every day, Jamie and I put a drop into our bucket. To raise the $15,000 Jamie needed to go to Everest, he did exactly what he said he would do. He sold his possessions, borrowed from his grandparents, Therese and Yvan Fournier, received a financial gift from his father and stepmother, and worked three jobs.

Jamie's day started at about 3:30 a.m. when he dragged himself out of bed to go to work as a traffic reporter for a local radio station. His on-air shift started at 4:30 a.m., by which time he had contacted police and fire officials, city road engineers and other sources of traffic information. His shift ended at 9 a.m. when he arrived at my apartment and spent the next 10 hours on the phone persevering through endless rejections by potential sponsors. Then he would train for a few hours before going on to his third job as a night DJ at a local bar. He'd inhale second-hand cigarette smoke there until the bar closed. A couple of hours of sleep brought him back to the beginning of the cycle.

Jamie has huge energy stores, both physically and mentally. And he absolutely never gives up.... He would carry you off a mountain even if both of his legs were broken. I trust him with my life.

In the midst of this frenetic schedule, although he was exhausted, Jamie never complained. He is a private man and it is often difficult for even those close to him to know how he is feeling. But when he commits to something, regardless of how he is feeling, he commits with everything he has. The result? He generates unbelievable momentum — not unlike a freight train. He is capable of pushing himself so hard he sometimes fails to see the energy "cliff" coming. Once past the point of no return, he can bottom out from exhaustion and illness.

When Jamie is operating on the safe side of his energy precipice, he is impressive to watch. He kept up his pre-Everest pace for the entire three months before we left. Incredibly, he still made time for a girlfriend, who, I am sure, was as amazed as I was with his personal strength. He has huge energy stores, both physically and mentally. And he absolutely never gives up. His body may fail him, but mentally, he is the toughest person I know. He would carry you off a mountain even if both of his legs were broken. I trust him with my life.

Our first joint challenge, aside from training, was to raise the $5,000 needed to ship our communications system to the mountain. Five weeks before departure, we still didn't have the money.

"What? Are you crazy?" prospective sponsors would tell us. "Why would anyone want to go to Mount Everest?"

"Do you guys have a death wish?"

"Communicate from Mount Everest? Nice idea, but... well... no."

"Sorry, it doesn't fit our mandate."

"Our budget's spent for this year."

"We'll get back to you."

"He'll get back to you."

"She'll get back to you."

"Someone may get back to you."

Two weeks before we were to leave for Everest, a story in the local newspaper read: "A Canadian climbing team's chances of broadcasting live from the top of Mount Everest this fall appear doomed."

Dealing with rejection and skepticism isn't easy. It is unpleasant and frustrating. Emotionally, it hurts. To cope, Jamie and I re-visited the power of our passions. We imagined ourselves standing in the wind on Everest, putting our reports off the mountain. It got us re-energized.

When the sponsor of the satellite system, AG Foods, learned we were strapped for cash, they decided the only way to realize any benefit from their involvement was to ensure the communications system got to the mountain. So, they increased their financial commitment. Just a week before departure, we had our money.

In the last week of July 1991, exhausted from the physical and organizational effort, we left North America. With his stepfather, Michael Keller, Jamie packaged, supported and shipped the U.S.-acquired satellite telecommunications system from Seattle. Then he left from there. I left from Calgary, where I had held the fort.

Dealing with rejection and skepticism isn't easy. It is unpleasant and frustrating. Emotionally, it hurts. To cope, Jamie and I re-visited the power of our passions.

All told, expedition leader Peter Austen and his 15-member North American team spent seven years organizing the $1 million "Climb for Hope" Everest Expedition. I spent two years on the communications system, three months of which were with Jamie. The expedition had nine tons of food, equipment, and supplies. The team left Vancouver for Kathmandu, Nepal, in a flurry of excitement and optimism.

The dream was about to take wing.

The Power of Passion

The Must of Trust

4

Once Peter's expedition arrived in Nepal, it didn't take long for our optimism to subside.

Clean running water, something we take for granted in the West, is often hard to come by in many parts of the world. Much of the water in Nepal, especially the water coming out of the taps, is polluted. You may be able to shower in it (although the running joke is "don't sing in the shower"), but you can't rinse your food in it, and you definitely can't drink it.

A bug probably got into Jamie's system through the food or an unlucky cup of tea. Three days after we arrived in Kathmandu, at 3 a.m., I was awakened by him vomiting into the waste basket in our hotel room. I got up, went to the bathroom, grabbed a face cloth and ran it under the tap. Then I rushed over to Jamie and held it to his forehead.

"Let 'er rip buddy," I said, trying to buoy his spirits, "Get that bug out of you."

When his vomiting finished, Jamie looked up at me haggard and sweating. Then he said: "You gotta love it."

It took a while before he explained what he meant:

"Being ill is a sign we're no longer dreaming of the adventure," he said. "We're living it — stomach bugs and all.

I'm actually quite ecstatic."

He added that the situation reminded him of something Franklin D. Roosevelt had said. It went something like: "The credit goes to the one who is in the arena, the one whose face is marred by blood and toil and sweat... and not to those poor and timid souls who know neither victory, nor defeat."

"The way I see it, we're in the arena," Jamie quipped. "We've made it to Kathmandu."

A few days later, with the help of antibiotics from our team doctor and climber, Denis Brown, Jamie's condition improved. When we got to Base Camp, I fell sick and Jamie took care of me.

From Kathmandu, the team's plan was to travel northeast for about 180 miles into ancient Tibet along a road the locals call "The Friendship Highway." The journey, which would have taken us about three hours on a North American highway, took a staggering three weeks. A day out of Kathmandu, The Friendship Highway became unfriendly. A series of mudslides swept the road into the Sun Kosi River below. We had to return to Kathmandu to re-think our strategy.

In our expedition planning, we had focused on the challenges we would face on the mountain. No one had thought that the monsoon rains, which came in early August, might produce

> *The credit goes to the one who is in the arena, the one whose face is marred by blood and toil and sweat... and not to those poor and timid souls who know neither victory, nor defeat.*
>
> — *Franklin D. Roosevelt*

mudslides long before we even saw Everest.

In life, mudslides come in many forms: cancer, heart disease, separation, divorce, layoff. For most of us, the most serious mudslide is death. The loss of a loved one, even a beloved pet, can shake the foundation of our lives and sweep us downward into depression.

En route to Everest, we had to figure out a way around our mudslides as quickly as possible — or risk bogging down in a sea of mud and disappointment. Our solution was to hire 400 Nepali porters to carry our nine tons of gear up and around the landslides. These porters appeared as if by magic from the surrounding villages. Each porter carried 85 to 90 pounds. That entire load was supported on a tump line — a band that went under the bottom of their loads and around their foreheads. They had no backpacks or ATVs to assist them. All they had was their own back and legs, a lifetime of load-carrying experience, and fiercely focused minds.

Each of the porters was paid about $10 USD a day. By North American standards, that sounds like a pittance, but the average annual income in Nepal is about $1,200 USD. That translates to a daily wage of about $3 USD. To the locals, our problem was a windfall.

Ninety pounds is a heavy load. It's like carrying more than 10 gallons of water. I weigh about 150 pounds. If you put 90 pounds on my back and I fell over, I'd have a hard time getting up.

We had a problem, however. One of our four communications boxes weighed 250 pounds — about the weight of a refrigerator. The contents of the box could not be reduced because the box contained delicate communications equipment. If we removed any of it, the contents could shake. If a single circuit board broke, or a tiny piece of soldering cracked, our entire communications dream could be in jeopardy.

We didn't know what to do. Without a road, we couldn't use a vehicle to move the box.

Before we could come up with a solution, one presented itself. Three tiny Nepali men, standing no more than 5-feet, 2-inches tall and 110 pounds each, appeared. Through an interpreter, they announced they could carry the box.

Jamie and I looked at each other and laughed. It seemed impossible that such small men could together even lift such a weight, let alone carry it up through the jungle in the rain. What's more, they were barefoot.

No, the interpreter insisted, the three porters would carry the box — one at a time.

We were at 10,000 feet. It was already becoming difficult to breathe normally. The underbrush was thick and almost impenetrable. The jungle crawled with leeches.

I tried to carry the box using a tump line. I made it about 30 feet. I felt like my head was going to rip from my shoulders.

— JAMIE —

The three porters — Dil, Ram and Zit — could carry the box. Each carried it for 15 minutes while one helped balance the load and the third rested.

They carried our box through some unbelievable conditions. Imagine, pouring monsoon rain, 90 degrees Fahrenheit, 100 per cent humidity, a hill in the jungle steeper than your average ski hill, no path, stinging nettle and mud under foot. With the weight of our dream on their backs, their legs shook under the strain. We watched wide-eyed as the mud oozed up between their toes. At times, because the ground was so steep, they had to stabilize themselves on all fours. Periodically, their bare feet slid backwards through the mud, but they never complained. Nor did they come close to dropping our box.

Incredibly, the three-man team moved so quickly they

passed the rest of us strolling along toting mere three pound fanny packs and umbrellas.

It wasn't the money that meant the most to them, although it was obviously important. What mattered most... was the pride they had in their work.

— ALAN —

As there was more than $100,000 USD of equipment in our box, we made chase after "our boys," but eventually, we couldn't keep up with them. Jamie and I personally paid Dil, Ram, and Zit at least double the regular rate. But it wasn't the money that meant the most to them, although it was obviously important. What mattered most, and what was communicated to us in actions and gestures, was the pride they had in their work. Clearly, they were the best porters in the region.

Dil, Ram, and Zit taught us a lesson about trust and teamwork we will never forget. They showed us that to achieve anything of significance in life, we have to share the load. We have to trust others to do their part while we do ours.

Letting go of control and trusting someone else to carry the ball is always an uncomfortable leap of faith. As human beings, we learn early how to take and keep control. We compete. As children, we learn about winning and losing — who gets the toy and who doesn't. When we become adults, we learn how to defeat others in everything from board games to boardrooms.

As athletes, the concept of competition has been hammered into Jamie and me. We have to work hard to keep from wanting to beat each other. Writing this book, blending together two different styles and points of view, has been a challenge. Cooperation is more complex than competition. It can take more time and effort, but in the end, it produces better results.

Dil, Ram and Zit also reminded us that what matters most is not what's outside us, but what's inside. They showed true inner strength and made a critically important contribution to our dream.

It took three days to move around the landslides and cross the border into Chinese-occupied Tibet. There, we bid good-bye to our three Supermen and said hello to Chinese Mountaineering Association officials with large army trucks. They presented us with a bill for $4,000 USD for delaying their trucks a week. We were once again reminded that climbing Everest is now a business.

Soon, the deluge of the monsoon gave way to the wind-blown desert of the arid Tibetan plateau above. At 14,000 feet, the carburetors of our specially-tuned trucks roared through the dust at 50 miles an hour.

In no time, our whole world changed. We found ourselves breathless not only from the altitude, but from our first views of the Himalayas and our first introduction to the culture of Tibet. We passed many Buddhist monasteries.

They showed us that to achieve anything of significance in life, we have to share the load. We have to trust others to do their part while we do ours.

One, located in the village of Xegar (pronounced JAY-GAR), was constructed on the side of a 16,000 foot peak. Thousands of handmade steps constructed over centuries using mud bricks ascended from the base of the mountain to its summit. There, tiny chambers where monks had once burned aromatic incense, chanted mantras and sought inner peace and enlightenment now lay in windswept ruin. Today, the main monastery is closer to the base of the mountain, where the effects of ultraviolet rays and parching winds are not so extreme.

The monks who began constructing the monastery knew they would not see its completion in their lifetime.

For Jamie, the monastery at Xegar highlighted a fundamental difference between East and West. The monks who began constructing the monastery knew they would not see its completion in their lifetime.

"How many of us would begin a project knowing we would never see its completion?" Jamie asks. "Few North Americans have goals hundreds of years in the future. Through our children, our living legacy, future goals can be achieved, but not by our own hands.

"Our Western culture is pinnacle-oriented. In Tibet and Nepal, much of the culture is process-oriented. They savor the journey. They live for the moment."

Eventually, after three weeks of travel, we arrived at the turnoff for Everest. Surprisingly, there was no road sign, no indication whatsoever we were about to turn toward the top of the world. We did. Several hours of rough road later, we rounded a bend and BOOM! Stretching skyward stood one of the seven wonders of the world — Everest.

The mountain's size is mind-boggling. None of the photographs, films, or written descriptions come close to capturing its immensity. It is absolutely massive. From its summit in the troposphere five and a half miles above sea level, three long ridges flare out, two for more than three miles. Together, they form the world's largest pyramid. The base of the mountain is so wide you cannot see it all from end to end. The towering north face stabs upward for 12,000 feet — more than two vertical miles. It is simultaneously an inspiring and intimidating sight.

When you drive to Base Camp, which you can do on the north side of the mountain, you look up at Everest. The hair stands up on the back of your neck, your stomach feels queasy, and your mouth goes dry. In an instant, you understand why Everest is called *Chomolungma*, the Tibetan word meaning "Mother Goddess of the World."

Everest has a pre-eminence and a presence you can feel. As you approach Base Camp, you get a feeling similar to stepping through the doors of a massive, high-ceilinged cathedral. You understand at some deep level you are being watched, and that you had best conduct yourself carefully.

There is no longer any doubt that Everest is the highest mountain on Earth. That fact has been definitively established using satellite measurements. It is 778 feet higher than the world's second tallest peak, K2, in the Karakoram Range of the Himalayas in Pakistan.

But when you stand in Base Camp, you don't need satellite measurements.

— JAMIE —

I've always thought Everest was more than rock or snow. It is something larger. Everest and other mountains represent nature's power and patience. Everest's greatness affects the souls of those who appreciate its majesty. The mountain is a reflection of our collective desire for personal greatness. When I climb, I try to join with the mountain. When I am in its presence, I am able to enhance my connectedness to my surroundings. I often find it

Our Western culture is pinnacle-oriented. In Tibet and Nepal, much of the culture is process-oriented. They savor the journey. They live for the moment.

easy to lose touch with this when I am in cities, in my office, or even when I am working with large groups. Everest helps me feel part of a larger whole.

Everest has a pre-eminence and a presence you can feel.... You understand at some deep level you are being watched, and that you had best conduct yourself carefully.

— ALAN —

As we pulled into Base Camp, our trucks bouncing along the highest road on Earth, we passed the Rongbuk Monastery at 16,500 feet, the highest permanently inhabited place on the planet. A few Buddhist monks waved hello. We responded with whoops of joy. Minutes later, after seven years of preparation, we arrived in Base Camp — a flat area covered with grass and gravel and strewn with boulders pushed forward by the Main Rongbuk Glacier that runs north from Everest.

Jubilant, Jamie and I jumped out, panting immediately from the altitude. We hugged. I felt a wave of emotion and satisfaction come over me.

The dream was no longer a dream.

We were face to face with Everest.

The Power of Passion

Overcoming Our Fear of Heights

5

Soon after arriving in Base Camp, all of us realized how poorly we felt physically.

"Some of us had extreme headaches," Jamie remembers, "the kind of headaches that hurt when you move your eyeballs."

At 17,000 feet, in Base Camp on Everest, the human body stops acclimatizing to the altitude. From there up, climbers deteriorate physically and mentally. An expedition is a race against time. You've got to get to the summit and back down again as quickly and as safely as possible before you develop potentially lethal high altitude sickness, or you fall, or succumb to the cold. On the north side, the summit is more than 13 miles away and 12,000 feet above you.

Seventeen thousand feet is higher than all but only a handful of mountains in North America. The partial pressure of the oxygen in the air, the pressure that forces the air back into our lungs after exhalation, is about one-half what it is at sea level. Because of this, the body's cells do not receive enough oxygen to regenerate. Each day you spend at Base Camp or above, you get weaker.

During an expedition, which usually lasts about two months, you experience a slow but steady decline in your physical and mental capacities. This downhill slide continues through summit day. On that day, the day when in theory you're supposed to need the most energy, you actually have the least.

At the summit, the partial pressure of the oxygen in the air is about one-third what it is at sea level. Near the summit, it can sometimes take up to two minutes to take a single step. It can take 15 to 30 seconds to mentally prepare for the step, a second to take it, a minute or so to recover from the exertion as you pant while draped over your ice ax, 15 seconds to recover from the exertion of standing up again, and finally, 15 to 30 more seconds to will yourself to take the next step.

Extreme altitude demands a fierce immediacy of focus. Everything you have, every ounce of energy, can be needed to move one foot six inches forward. Sometimes, it's as if you must squeeze out that step through a tiny hole in your soul.

The altitude is the biggest challenge on Everest. Throw in unpredictable weather, hurricane-force winds that can tear tents apart like tissue paper, windchills off the scale of most human experience, intense interpersonal stresses that can bring climbers to blows and you begin to understand the agony of Everest. One climber wrote: "Mountaineering is the art of suffering." On Everest, that suffering can include death. For every four climbers who have made it to the summit, one has died trying somewhere on the

> *Everything you have, every ounce of energy, can be needed to move one foot six inches forward. Sometimes, it's as if you must squeeze out that step through a tiny hole in your soul.*

The Power of Passion

mountain.

Once we'd arrived in Base Camp, fear set in. We realized how difficult it was just to walk 50 feet across camp. We took our heart rates (usually about 60 beats a minute at sea level). Some were racing as high as 120. Even when we lay down, they stayed high — between 90

If we feel this badly now, how is this team ever going to get all the way up there and back down again safely?

and 110. We panted from the exertion of rolling over in our sleeping bags. We felt weak and frail, like we had instantly aged 40 years. Some of us were nauseous.

A climbing friend of mine once said: "Being at high altitude is like growing old very fast. You don't eat well, you don't sleep well, and you don't feel well."

In the midst of this discomfort, we somehow had to operate. At first, I wasn't able to do much more than help set up camp and walk around. It took the longest time to complete the simplest tasks — like getting dressed in the morning, or collecting water from the glacial stream nearby.

In this pre-acclimatized state, Jamie and I looked up at the summit of Everest towering above us. We swallowed hard. We asked ourselves: "If we feel this badly now, how is this team ever going to get all the way up there and back down again safely?" Fear took hold. "What if we don't make it to the top?" "What if we do, but we can't make it down?" "What if we lose fingers and toes to frostbite?" "What if someone dies?" "What if I die?"

All of these fears raise the obvious question, the one we are so often asked as climbers...

"Why?"

Jamie and I can't tell you how many times we've been asked:

"Are you crazy?"

"Do you have a death wish?

"Are you nuts?"

The answer is "no" to all these questions.

After meeting hundreds of "risk-takers" over the years, we believe there are as many reasons climbers climb as there are climbers. As a whole, however, these reasons appear to have little to do with death, danger, thrill-seeking or adrenaline rushes. Nor do they have much to do with "Because it's there" either. Those words were said by British mountaineer George Leigh Mallory. He was being pestered by a reporter as to why he climbed and after numerous unsuccessful attempts to explain his motives, he gave up in disgust and walked away. As he did, he uttered the now famous words. They have stuck because they are simple, but they are simply not the reason climbers climb.

I adventure for many reasons. One is to attempt to overcome my past failures, to prove something to myself, something I will never be able to prove. None of us can change our past.

The second reason I adventure is to achieve what I feel is my full physical potential. The third reason is to positively affect others through public speaking. Everest gets people's attention. Once you have that, you can say something.

I only seem to get satisfaction out of things that require me to reach well beyond myself. If climbing Everest was easy, everyone would do it. The fact that it's difficult makes it worth doing.

> *If climbing Everest was easy, everyone would do it. The fact that it's difficult makes it worth doing.*

Jamie and I believe that part of the answer to the question "Why?" has to do with something we all share as human beings. It has to do with curiosity.

When we learn to walk, the

first thing we want to do is cross the room, pick up that object on the coffee table and stick it in our mouths. We want to touch it, feel it, taste it and experience it. Exploration is an instinct. It is as instinctive as play. In fact, it is a form of play.

Entrepreneurs are like explorers. They are curious to see if they can make a better widget, penetrate a new market, or "beat" the competition. Jamie and I believe the desire to make money is only part of what motivates most business people, although for some it is a large part. We believe curiosity, the desire to know more, is the larger driving force. Some people are attracted to the unknown.

A sense of curiosity and child-like wonder produces what Jamie and I call "wonderlust." Unfortunately, as we get older, some of us gradually get programmed away from our exploration instinct. We are bombarded with so many negative messages about the poor economy, declining employment opportunities, downsizing, civil unrest, bombings, wars, marriage breakup, government cutbacks, political crises, layoffs and on and on, that a pallor of gloom can descend. Coupled with this are what Jamie and I call "The Terrible Toos" we sometimes hear from others — that we are too short to play basketball, too tall to be beautiful, too fat to become fit or too mathematically-challenged to be a physicist.

These two sources of negativity — what we are told about our world and what we are told about ourselves, can gradually erode our self-confidence. If this erosion is not checked, we can begin to believe there's no sense trying anymore. We give up on our goals. We abandon our dreams. We stop hoping and we start fearing.

In Base Camp, we started fearing.

"It took $1 million in fund-raising and seven years of effort by Peter and his team to get us there," Jamie recalls. "They transported all this gear to the mountain and got all the support from suppliers and sponsors. But when we got there, my legs started to shake just looking up at Everest. I joked, 'Whoa, well, let's just take some pictures and get the heck out of here.'

"I was afraid we might not make it. The intensity of the fear was paralyzing. It created something of a psychological paralysis in Al too."

We don't have to go to Mount Everest to find fear. The most pervasive fear in the West today is a fear of the unknown, particularly of the future — a fear of losing job security, or of losing a job altogether. "How are we going to provide for our families?" "Will we have a job tomorrow?" "What if we get laid off?"

Questions of this kind are faced by all of us, even the first Canadian to climb Mount Everest, Laurie Skreslet. He has a philosophy about fear. He maintains: "When we run away from fear, it gets bigger, but when we advance towards it, it shrinks." Today, fear is the number one thing that stops us from achieving our dreams, or becoming more fulfilled. Despite continued unhappiness, some of us do not quit our unfulfilling, low paying jobs, start our own business, or look for different work because we're afraid we might go broke. We can't bear the thought of leaving one job without having another job to go to, or we think we just can't make the financial or psychological leap.

> *When we got there, my legs started to shake just looking up at Everest. I joked, 'Whoa, well, let's just take some pictures and get the heck out of here.'*

Jamie and I believe we expend a tremendous amount of energy and time "looking down." We focus on those things we cannot control, instead of focusing on those things we can control. We focus on falling, or more accurately, on our fear of falling.

When I started rock climbing, I was afraid of heights. I climbed up just fine, but as soon as I looked down, I felt queasy and light-headed. I disliked hanging out on narrow ledges and I rarely enjoyed the view. The view, as I saw it, only accentuated the fact that I was a long way off the ground. If I fell, I knew what the outcome could be.

Through climbing, I have learned to manage my fear of heights. It no longer bothers me to be in high places. I have learned that it is only useful to look down when you need to see where you are putting your feet.

Jamie and I believe we expend a tremendous amount of energy and time "looking down." We focus on those things we cannot control, instead of focusing on those things we can control.

On Everest, we devised a strategy for coping with fear.

"We tried to focus on little things," Jamie says, "like sharpening our ice axs. That took our minds off the enormity of Everest for a moment, and enabled us to take a small step. Once we took a step, it was natural for us to take another one. That broke the paralysis and got us moving."

On a boulder in Base Camp, we took another step — a team picture. There were 15 Canadians and five Nepali Sherpas.

The Sherpas are the mountain people of Nepal, a country that runs roughly west to east for about 500 miles between the northeastern border of India and the southern frontier of China. Despite its size, Nepal is home to eight of the world's 14 tallest peaks, among them Everest herself. While the Tibetans call Everest Chomolungma — the Mother Goddess of the World, the Sherpas call her Sagarmatha, Forehead in the Sky.

Not to be confused with porters like Dil, Ram and Zit who carry loads at lower elevations, or guides who accompany tourists on Himalayan treks, the Sherpas are the finest high altitude climbers in the world. The hallmark of the Sherpas is their amazing ability to move swiftly at high altitude while carrying heavy loads. They are as much at home in the thin air of the Himalayas as we are in our own living rooms in the West.

As Jamie and I lay in our tents in Base Camp, we did not feel like Sherpas. In addition to struggling with the altitude, we also had to deal with the fear that our communications system would fail. What if the satellite telephone didn't work? What would the sponsors say? What would Peter Austen say? What would we say?

Eventually, the time came to face our fear. When everything was ready, we started our gasoline-powered electrical generator and hooked up the satellite telephone. Then we fixed the satellite dish at the proper angle to make contact with the satellite 22,500 miles up in space. After a few deep breaths, we crossed our fingers and prepared to make our own "summit" bid.

I remember Jamie handing me the telephone receiver and saying, "Here buddy, dial tone to anywhere in the world!"

We decided to call my parents in Ottawa, in eastern Canada. First, we had to go through the satellite receiving station in Perth, Australia.

I almost dropped the receiver when a thickly-accented voice answered matter-of-factly:

"Gidday. This is Inmarsat Australia."

"My God," I thought. "This phone actually works."

Fumbling, I explained we wanted to call Canada.

"No problem, mate. Please hold for a moment."

We waited...

"It's ringing," said the operator in Perth. "Have a great day."

He hung up.

I listened to the phone ring half a world away. The anticipation was unbelievable. Jamie was visibly bubbling too. Were we actually going to do it? Would our system actually work?

The phone rang once, twice, three times. "Come on folks," I said, "answer the phone. We're calling from Everest."

Finally, on the fourth ring, it was picked up. My heart jumped...

I understood for the first time since losing the national gymnastics championships what winning really meant. It wasn't the destination. It was the journey. I was elated.

We got their answering machine.

There we were expecting this fabulous summit experience after we had struggled so hard on our climb, and whoosh, out went the air from our balloon. After savoring the irony of it for a moment, we hung up.

Jamie and I hugged. I slapped him on the back and together, we celebrated a victory we had worked so hard to create. We had achieved the first of our two communications goals — to establish a live telephone link from the top of the world. I understood for the first time since losing the national gymnastics championships what winning really meant. It wasn't the destination. It was the journey. I was elated.

It took about an hour for the enormity of it to sink in. I went into the kitchen tent, made myself a big mug of hot chocolate and sat and drank it with one of the Sherpas.

"Congratulations, Alan," said Ang Temba. "You and Jamie have done well."

Tears started to roll down my face. I was overcome with emotion.

That night, I wrote in my diary:

"I can't sleep tonight. I'm too excited. This was my first Everest."

There would be others.

The Triumph in a Team

6

After about 10 days in Base Camp, our bodies adjusted to the altitude to the degree they could and we gradually began to feel better. Although we still had occasional headaches, our nausea largely passed. During this preliminary acclimatization period, our blood thickened with more oxygen-carrying red blood cells. To dilute the blood and reduce the risk of stroke and other circulatory problems, we each began drinking up to a gallon of water a day. We joked that if anyone lost their way on the mountain, we could always find them by following the yellow brick road.

At this point, many of our 20 team members began making the long, 13-mile trek to Advance Base Camp at 21,300 feet. Advance Base Camp is more than 1,000 feet higher than the highest point in North America, the summit of Alaska's Mount McKinley, at 20,320 feet. On Everest, it is not until you are higher than this that the real climbing begins.

— JAMIE —

On the north side of Everest, climbers use yaks to transport their heavier gear across the rugged moraine between Base Camp and Advance Base Camp. Yaks are high altitude cattle. They can carry up to 120 pounds at a time to altitudes of up to 22,000 feet, but they are also rather skittish around climbers, whose smell apparently offends them. Since yaks sport foot-long horns, climbers tend to keep their distance from yaks too.

Yaks are kept by yak herders — the nomadic people of Tibet. One day, I was invited to spend a night with the yak herders. I hoped to observe first-hand how they survived in the harsh, high altitude environment with so few resources. I also wanted to foster a sense of team camaraderie. As none of the herders spoke English, I thought that if we couldn't communicate their importance to us in words, we should do it through actions. They were, after all, part of our team the way Dil, Ram and Zit were.

The yak herders carry everything they own on their backs. They've fashioned most of what they own by hand. They don't have all the high-tech gear we have — the propane/butane stoves, the down parkas and all the flashy colors. Their tents are made from yak hair, so is their clothing. They eat yak meat, yak cheese, yak butter and yak milk. They even burn yak dung for heating and cooking.

Imagine the kind of fire you get when you burn manure — a whole lot of smoke and not a whole lot of flame. Because my visit was a rather festive occasion, they went to great lengths to collect enough manure to keep me warm that night. Before we bedded down, they collected all the dry dung they could in a bucket. Then they brought it into the tent and lit it on fire. Because I was their guest, they gave me what they considered to be the best seat in the house — curled up right beside the yak dung fire.

There was smoke everywhere. My eyes burned all night. I probably cried about half a quart of water. I slept little and coughed and wheezed a lot.

The next morning, after saying my good-byes, I

staggered out of the tent. As the smoke cleared from my eyes, I realized my relationship with those once-skittish yaks had changed. Now, they walked right up to me. Now, I could pet them. One older yak at first looked at me like he might charge, but then stopped suddenly and sniffed me. Then, he actually licked me. It was a moment of bonding.

The smoke and smell of the yak dung fire crystallized a feeling into a conviction. As I carried the dung's acrid smell in my clothes and hair, I reflected

I must be willing to eat and sleep with them on their cold ground. There, close to the earth, I have discovered greater understanding. This is one of the many gifts these people offer.

on the experience and others like it I have enjoyed in countries like Madagascar, Tanzania and Turkey. A considerable part of Everest's attraction is being among the local people and learning from them and their ways. For me, it is not possible to do this from afar because I am saturated with the too-familiar smells of my own culture. I must bathe myself in the pungency of theirs. I have to move to their rhythms. I need to build rapport that lies beyond language, in gestures filled with honest intention. Above all, I must be willing to eat and sleep with them on their cold ground. There, close to the earth, I have discovered greater understanding. This is one of the many gifts these people offer.

— ALAN —

With the help of the yaks and yak herders, we established Advance Base Camp about a week later. Once our communications tent was erected there, our next challenge was to stage our first press conference. Jamie had to descend to Base Camp and set up the technical infrastructure.

The conference was scheduled for 10:15 p.m. Jamie had less than 10 hours to descend, marry the handheld radio system we would be using on the upper mountain with our satellite telephone in Base Camp and give the entire communications system its first full-blown test. It was to be one of the most challenging days of Jamie's life.

— JAMIE —

To make the deadline, I had to almost jog down the mountain. After my four-hour descent, I had three hours left.

I went to work in a frenzy. With 30 minutes to zero hour, I was still having major technical difficulties. I couldn't establish a connection between the radios and the telephone. During testing in North America, the equipment had worked fine, but the journey to Base Camp had caused some damage. With the soldering iron glowing in the dark, and with just five minutes left, as if by magic, everything fell into place. The press conference went off without a hitch.

When we finally wrapped things up, it was about 1:00 a.m. I remember stepping out of the communications tent. There was no one around. Everyone was higher on the mountain. It was dark and windy and I was hungry, so I made my way to the kitchen tent. There, by the light of my headlamp, I managed to find a can of tuna. In my fatigue, I couldn't find a can opener so I used a screwdriver to punch holes in the lid. Then, I sucked back the juice.

Euphoria came over me. I felt such a deep sense of pride at having done what we had set out to do, yet there were no crowds, no cheering. There was only me and that stinky can of tuna.

I realized something in that kitchen tent, on that night in

the dark on Everest. What I realized was that real winning had nothing to do with beating someone else, or crossing the finish line first, or standing on top. Winning wasn't anything external at all. It was an internal satisfaction, a deep inner sense of pride and joy. Success can only be measured within ourselves, by ourselves. It has nothing to do with other people's perception of our achievements. It has everything to do with our own perceptions of our efforts.

What I realized was that real winning had nothing to do with beating someone else, or crossing the finish line first, or standing on top. Winning wasn't anything external at all. It was an internal satisfaction, a deep inner sense of pride and joy.

— ALAN —

In Advance Base Camp, I too was alone. The tiny communications tent was so jammed with communications equipment I couldn't even stand up to cheer. So I just lay back and savored the moment. After a minute or two, I shut off the radio and went outside the tent.

To my right, the northeast ridge of Everest swept down beside the east Rongbuk Glacier like a snow-covered serpent. Behind me, the ominous North Col slope rose up from the glacier in towering majesty. To my left, the sheer rock wall of Everest's northern sister, Mount Changtse, jutted skyward for about 1,000 feet. It was a spectacular scene that underscored the poignancy of our achievement.

But Jamie and I were not together. That felt odd. It felt cold and empty. To have worked so closely as a team and yet not be together to share the victory left me feeling sad.

It was anti-climactic. I hadn't realized until then how much doing it together had made the experience meaningful. He felt joyous. I felt empty. What we did share was the solitude, and the silence.

Days passed before Jamie and I were finally able to get together. By then, the magic of the moment had given way to fresh new challenges. We never celebrated together. We should have.

What had been monsoon rain on the approach to Base Camp became snow at Advance Base Camp. Our team found itself wading through waist and chest deep snow struggling to establish Camp Four at 23,500 feet.

Perched on top of the North Col between Everest and Changtse, Camp Four stands at the top of the 2,000-foot high North Col slope. Over the years, some 70 people have died on the slope, more fatalities than on any other feature on the mountain, including the deadly Khumbu Icefall on the mountain's south side in Nepal. Not only does the slope have a perfect steepness for producing avalanches, but it is also riddled with deep crevasses and huge ice blocks the size of three and four-story apartment buildings. Mountaineers call these ice blocks "seracs."

To make the slope's lethal character even more sinister, it faces east. A few hours after the first rays of the sun strike it, it becomes a frying pan of ultraviolet rays and searing heat. It is not uncommon to register temperatures on the slope in excess of 90 degrees Fahrenheit. High altitude peaks are always cold at night, but during the day, because of the altitude, there is little atmosphere to filter out the sun's ultraviolet rays. Thus, peaks like Everest can become exceptionally hot, especially below about 23,000 feet.

To help ferry loads from Advance Base Camp to Camp Four, our team anchored rope up the North Col slope. Time and again, avalanches either swept the rope off the route or snowfalls buried it so deeply it took many hours to extricate. It was two weeks before we were finally able to establish Camp Four.

Camps on Everest are not pre-established. To create them, climbers must painstakingly carry loads of equipment from the camp below. By the time you have climbed Everest this way, you have climbed between 18 and 22 vertical miles — the

Teamwork has been one of the hallmarks of Everest expeditions since the mountain was first climbed in 1953.

equivalent of climbing Everest eight to ten times. Expeditions expend large amounts of energy just establishing and stocking their camps. Once these camps are in place, climbers have to expend more energy maintaining them. It is a huge team effort.

Teamwork has been one of the hallmarks of Everest expeditions since the mountain was first climbed in 1953. Only three days before Hillary and Tenzing made it to the top on May 29, two now-forgotten climbers called Charles Evans and Tom Boudillon left Everest's South Col (Col is the French word for mountain saddle) at 26,000 feet. They climbed to just 300 vertical feet from the top. There, realizing they did not have enough daylight or oxygen left to make it to the summit and back again safely, they cached oxygen bottles for Hillary and Tenzing and returned exhausted to the Col.

"(Evans and Bourdillon) returned to give the next pair the incalculable benefit of their experience," expedition leader, Lord John Hunt, wrote, "and of their confidence that the true crest could yet be ours."

It was during my first carry to the crest of the North Col slope that I came to know in small measure the exhaustion Evans and Bourdillon had felt. One crisp September morning at about 23,000 feet, I found myself face first in the snow on all fours, panting uncontrollably and on the verge of vomiting.

As my heart raced and I gasped for air, the massive North Col slope loomed around me. Below, it fell 2,000-feet to the East Rongbuk Glacier. Above, huge seracs teetered on the edge of reality. They clung to the face, threatening at any moment to "calf off" and crush me.

I cannot recall a more humbling moment in my adventure experiences. Despite years of heavy training, I believed, wrongly, that I was ready for Everest. After all, Jamie and I had carried those 85-pound packs up and down that dingy stairwell day in and day out for hours. I had supplemented this training with marathon runs up to 26 miles long.

Nothing you read or hear can prepare you for the sudden shock of exertion at high altitude. Even the most physically fit climbers can be reduced to gasping weaklings. This is always the way it is for Jamie and me, particularly in the early stages of any expedition. Things always get better, but first they are, well... bad.

My agony seemed interminable. First, I'd drag myself up from the snow. Then, I'd squeeze out two or three excruciatingly slow steps, drop to all fours panting uncontrollably and come face to face with the cold reality of my own inadequacy.

> **Nothing you read or hear can prepare you for the sudden shock of exertion at high altitude. Even the most physically fit climbers can be reduced to gasping weaklings.**

Suddenly, my panting was interrupted:

"Good morning, Alan!" said a chipper voice. "Are you okay?"

Like a scared rabbit with its head partially buried between

The Power of Passion

its legs, I peered out behind me. I was amazed to see the first of our Sherpas strolling casually up the slope like they were at a Sunday picnic.

"Yeah... (breath)... yeah... (breath)," I managed to squeeze out.

"Good," replied Da Nuru, a veteran of several Everest expeditions. Like most Sherpas who have climbed with mountaineers from all over the world, he spoke several languages, including English.

In a moment, he and his companions blasted by me. Without missing a step, they dispensed with the traditional jumar braking devices normally used to move safely up the anchored rope. Instead, they batmanned effortlessly hand-over-hand up the rope like kids pulling in perch. The contrast of Westerner-cum-whimp and Sherpa supermen was made even more dramatic by the fact that I knew the Sherpas were carrying packs more than twice the weight of mine.

It took me many more hours of discomfort until I finally reached Camp Four. A few days later, I managed to corner one of the Sherpas, Ang Temba. He had summitted Everest the previous spring as part of the first Sherpa expedition to the mountain. I asked him why it had taken his people almost 40 years after Sir Edmund Hillary and Sherpa Tenzing Norgay's ascent in 1953 to finally launch an Everest expedition themselves in 1991. Everest was, after all, in their backyard.

His reply was surprising:

"We didn't need to climb Everest," he explained quietly.

"Why not?" I asked. "It's right here. You're right here. All you have to do is climb it."

He looked back at me like I didn't know anything (which, of course, I didn't). Then he paused before speaking:

"Everest is beautiful and it's there," he said calmly. "What more do you need?"

The Triumph in a Team 53

The Sherpas brought far more than load carrying ability to our team. They brought balance and perspective.

With the help of our Sherpas, our team pushed up the north ridge above Camp Four and put in Camp Five at 25,500 feet. There, however, we ran into another challenge. While descending from Camp Five after depositing a load there, one of our climbers, Tim Rippel, twisted his knee so badly he couldn't walk.

"All I remember was taking a step," Tim recalls. "My right leg just poked right through the top crust of the snow to my knee. I had my pack on and it twisted me sideways.

"Mario (Mario Bilodeau, a fellow team member) said he heard a loud popping noise. Right away, it felt like my knee was on fire. I slid down the slope for about 15 feet on my back and I knew I wasn't going anywhere. I couldn't even straighten my leg."

Mario, and other team members John McIsaac and Myk Kurth, together with some of the team's Sherpas, dragged Tim through the snow back to Camp Four. Because of excruciating pain, he could not descend the North Col slope under his own power. We would have to lower him on a rope all the way down the slope — a prospect that excited none of us, least of all Tim.

"When I got to Camp Four, a lot ran through my mind," Tim recalls. "Am I going to be able to walk again? I had injured the same knee six years earlier in a ski accident... I knew the expedition was over for me. Years of planning and climbing... I felt like I had let down part of the team and myself."

> "Everest is beautiful and it's there, what more do you need?"
>
> — Ang Temba

The last thing we wanted to do was lower Tim down the North Col slope in the heat of the day. With the slope loaded with wet snow, that was tantamount to putting a gun to his head, and to ours. The avalanche hazard was too high. So, we started early.

A rescue like this takes time. The injured climber has to be moved slowly but carefully over seracs and across crevasses and avalanche chutes. Even if we started at midnight, we knew we would probably still be lowering Tim down the face by mid-morning. If we didn't have him off the slope by noon, the avalanche hazard could make things dicey.

Our climbing leader, Ross Cloutier, coordinated the rescue. It was nerve-wracking. First, we anchored rope at the top of the Col on which to lower Tim. Next, climber Pat Morrow and two of our Sherpas climbed halfway up the face to receive him. From there, they would relay him the rest of the way.

The rescue was not without its challenges. Pat fell into a crevasse and nearly choked to death when he became entangled in his safety rope. Only fast thinking and some free-hanging gymnastics saved his life. He managed to crawl out safely.

Tim was largely unaware of what was going on. He had torn ligaments in his knee and had received a large dose of painkillers to dull the pain. While Jamie monitored the situation from Base Camp, I took photographs from high on the slope. Three years later, under Tim's direction, Jamie would be called upon to coordinate a similar rescue himself.

At times, Tim, attached to a climbing harness and packed into a sleeping bag, dangled freely in space as he was lowered over the top of overhanging seracs. Like some kind of limp human potato sack, his life hung from the thread of the rope. His drug-induced stupor only compounded the situation because we knew if he got stuck at any point, it would be difficult, if not impossible, for him to extricate himself. He was alone in a dangerous place, relying totally on us to get him down safely.

"All I remember was going down the slope and things just started getting steeper and steeper," Tim recalls. "I remember looking at the snow slope around me and thinking, 'I could ski this.'

"Then, I had a semi-blackout. I remember going over a little vertical pitch... But I still think I could have skied that."

The rescue took many hours, but eventually we got Tim to the bottom of the slope. There, he was met by a small army of rescuers who loaded him onto a makeshift sled fashioned from one of the team's aluminum cooking boxes and a pair of skis. Dr. Denis Brown gave him a shot of morphine. Minutes later, Tim lost consciousness.

"I remember waking up as the guys wrestled me into my tent at Advance Base Camp," Tim says. "Denis looked at my knee and said I was out of there."

For Tim, the pain of that diagnosis was more difficult emotionally than physically. Tim is a superb team player and a driven climber. It was like taking a star player out of the World Series in the ninth inning of the final game.

The team now had a transportation problem. How were we to get Tim the 13 miles to Base Camp? It would have been a tremendous effort to carry him. Someone suggested a yak might be better. Then, Jamie's smoky night team-building with the yak herders paid off in spades. With their help, we strapped Tim on the back of a user-friendly yak for a two-day-long evacuation to Base Camp. This later became known to John Ingle Travel, our travel insurance sponsor, as the famous Everest "Yak Evac."

"It was the most interesting ride I've ever had in my life," Tim recalls of the journey during which he spent 15 hours on the back of a yak. "I had excruciating pain and terrible saddle sores. The first day, the three yak herders tied my legs together underneath the animal. They wanted to make sure I didn't fall off. But that really aggravated my injury.

"The yak was amazing. There were a few places on the trail where we had to cross a little ridge of rock or ice. Every once in a while, the animal slipped. I found myself looking at a 35-foot drop to a rock pile. I thought, 'Please don't fall.' I had to fully trust the animal because there was no way I could bail off.

"The yak was very pleasant. It could have tossed me off like a bronc, but it never did. It was pretty gentle. Wherever it had a tricky move to make, it would pause for a split second and figure the moves out, like a climber. It was really cool. The animal was surprisingly graceful."

The thing that stays with me about Tim's rescue is that when there's a crisis, everyone has to work together. There's no room for in-fighting or argument. The job has to be done. On Everest, it meant Tim's life. It was a true team triumph.

"During his yak ride, Tim said there was some kind of bizarre non-verbal communication that took place between him and the yak," Jamie recalls. "As they descended, they passed many huge boulders. Tim said he noticed that although the animal allowed his uninjured knee to brush these boulders, it never once allowed his injured knee to touch."

When they eventually made it down to Base Camp, a strange thing happened. The yak herders unstrapped Tim from the back of the yak and placed him on the ground. Then, the two of them stared at each other.

"It just felt like it was telling me, 'Okay, you're safe. Now that I've done what they brought me up here for, I'm going home. I wish you all the best for your trip home.'

"I'm sure that was what was on its mind. It was certainly what was on my mind."

From Base Camp, Tim was transported by truck and bus to Kathmandu where he flew back to Canada. Although surgery was not required, he was told to stay off his feet.

"The thing that stays with me about Tim's rescue is that when there's a crisis, everyone has to work together," Jamie recalls. "There's no room for in-fighting or argument. The job has to be done. On Everest, it meant Tim's life. It was a true team triumph."

Victory Through Effort

7

After the human setback of Tim's injury, we were soon faced with a mechanical one. Our gasoline-powered electrical generator in Advance Base Camp broke down. With the aid of Jamie's yak herder friends, we loaded up a yak in Base Camp with a back-up generator and sent it up to Advance Base Camp. Jamie joined me there a few days later with the machine. His arrival would prove providential. For the two of us, it sparked the biggest crisis of the expedition.

Because we had lost valuable time in the rescue, it was decided at a team meeting in Advance Base Camp that only eight of our 15 North American climbers would continue higher on the mountain. Before the expedition, Peter had agreed that provided our communications commitments were met, Jamie and I should have the status of climbers. Because Jamie had spent most of the expedition in Base Camp manning the communications system, he had deteriorated less from the altitude than I had at Advance Base Camp. Ross Cloutier, our climbing leader, selected Jamie to carry loads to 26,000 feet. But not wanting to come between us, he left it to us to decide who would climb higher.

I remember coming out of that meeting and bursting into tears. It was so disappointing. I wanted to climb higher. To prepare for the expedition, I had climbed three high altitude peaks in Mexico as well as Mount McKinley, the highest peak in North America. Jamie, by contrast, had no high altitude climbing experience.

It was dusk in Advance Base Camp and the wind was blowing up the moraine. I stared up at the summit of Everest and I felt utterly alone. I'd come up short — again. Just then, Jamie came out of the kitchen tent.

— JAMIE —

In the gathering darkness, I could just make out the shape of Al. For the longest time, he couldn't speak. So, I just knelt beside him.

A long time passed before he could say anything. Finally, I asked: "Do you feel you've failed?"

He said "Yes."

I thought, how could this be failure? We took $250,000 worth of communications gear (one box alone contained about $100,000 worth of equipment and there were three others) halfway around the world to the middle of nowhere, got it to work, carried loads to 23,500 feet, helped save Tim's life, gave it all we had and that is failure?

Success isn't standing on the podium, or hearing the cheers of others, or standing on the summit at all. It's giving it your all.

I looked up at the stars coming out over Everest. The stars there are unbelievable. You're so high and there's no light from any town. I looked at one star in particular, the brightest one. For the first time in my life, it all started to make sense. As I held Al while he wept, my cross-country skiing experiences, that first press conference and Tim's rescue distilled into a realization.

Success isn't standing on the podium, or hearing the cheers of others, or standing on the summit at all. It's giving it your all, like Al had, or caring for others the way the team and yak herders had during Tim's rescue.

We have such a narrow view of success. It's like Al was using a telescope to look at only one star. He saw the star all right, but he was missing the galaxy of other successes he'd had around it. I tried to explain that to Al.

— ALAN —

I heard the words, but I didn't understand them at that moment. I was too focused on my own little world. I wanted to climb higher. I felt like I still had energy left, but Jamie was healthier. Considering he had never climbed anything higher than 10,000 feet before, he had a huge opportunity. He could go from the Canadian Rockies to high on Everest in one step.

— JAMIE —

So there we were. Al wanted to continue. I had the opportunity. But one of us had to go down to Base Camp to operate the communications system. One of us had to turn his back on further climbing.

At first we sat there calmly on the moraine in the approaching darkness, a couple of friends talking quietly about what to do. Each of us presented our case.

Gradually, things started to get heated. Then, they got out of control. We started to argue. Tempers flared. An hour and a half later, I caught myself looking down at the rocks on the moraine for one I could pick up and throw at Al. Luckily, they were too big because if they hadn't been, Al and I might not be here today. It sounds ridiculous, but remember, we're two guys at 21,000 feet on Everest. We've been on the mountain for over a month. We've lost a lot of weight, been sick, worked hard, and we haven't slept properly the whole time. We're right on the edge.

— ALAN —

Our egos really surfaced then, along with our fatigue and frustration. I wanted to plow Jamie, just let him have it — full in the face, full on, with everything I had left. We had worked so hard, but I wanted to continue climbing and Jamie wanted to continue climbing — who was going to climb higher? Like a couple of bighorn sheep, we collided head on.

Finally, I did the only thing I could do, aside from kill Jamie. I called a 10-minute truce.

Ten minutes passed, but I still didn't have an answer. I just sat there, frustrated and afraid. By now, it was dark.

Then, the strangest thing happened. I felt this hand alight on my shoulder. I turned around and Jamie was standing there. He had this serene look on his face, like he'd figured it all out... and he had.

This is what he said:

"Alan, this communications system is your baby. This is your dream. I'm only here because you helped me get here. So, for the sake of our friendship, I want you to go up and see how high you can go. Because when you're old and gray, when you can't climb mountains anymore, I want you to look back on this moment with no regret. There must be no dishonor. Our friendship is what counts most here. And it counts more than any piece of rock."

> *I want you to look back on this moment with no regret. There must be no dishonor. Our friendship is what counts most here.*

— JAMIE —

Since then, many people have asked me what led to my decision. As I sat there on the moraine, I started thinking about how I'd felt on the podium as a ski racer. Why was I missing something there? And I thought: what happens if I get up this mountain and then I remember my friend is 12,000 feet below, denied the opportunity to be up there with me. How would I feel then? How fulfilled would I be?

He made a huge personal sacrifice on behalf of our two-man team. He put my dreams ahead of his own. I will always be grateful for that.

For me, the decision that had taken hours of raging energy to make was really quite simple.

— ALAN —

The next morning, Jamie headed down the mountain. It was an emotional parting.

Somehow, Jamie saw the larger picture, the panoramic view. He made a huge personal sacrifice on behalf of our two-man team. He put my dreams ahead of his own. I will always be grateful for that. I think he was paying me back for the two years I had worked by myself to get the communications system started and for having lobbied to get him on the team with just a few months to go. Jamie is very conscious of checks and balances. He knows when to call in a favor and when to give one. I like that about him.

I don't feel guilty about the decision I made. I recognize what Jamie did for me. He recognizes what I did for him. We got through it and our friendship became stronger.

By now, our expedition was running behind schedule. Because of delays caused by the mudslides, the heavy snows and Tim's rescue, the summit weather window was starting to close. Winter was fast approaching.

We did not want to be on Everest when winter arrived. With it would come winds of over 60 miles an hour. The summit of Everest is one of the few places in the world where the jet stream touches the Earth. When it does, it scours the upper reaches of the mountain and blasts anyone or anything there into oblivion. Although there have been ascents of Everest in winter, all have returned with dreadful stories of frostbite and suffering.

In the closing days of the expedition, I climbed to Camp Four at 23,500 feet, but could go no higher. I had simply expended too much energy on the communications system before and during the expedition. I learned that on Everest, you can only wear one hat.

At another team meeting, we whittled the expedition down to our three strongest climbers: John McIsaac, Denis Brown and Mario Bilodeau. It is usually obvious who comprises the summit team. They are the strongest ones, the healthiest ones and sometimes, they are the only ones left standing.

Of the trio, John McIsaac was one of the most driven.

— JAMIE —

I first met John in the stairwell of a downtown office tower in Calgary in late 1991. Alan staged a stair climb competition as a fund raiser for the 1991 expedition and John and I were among the volunteers. He seemed calm, yet intense, a good combination for a climber. I liked him right away and my respect for him grew during the 1991 climb. He kept an eye on me during that expedition and on my first carry to the North Col, he took me under his wing. I respected his sense for when to be strong and when to be tender. During a tough day in the mountains, I witnessed his hard side. He was powerful. When I saw John with his two daughters, I saw his soft and compassionate side. I liked the contrast.

— ALAN —

John, Denis, and Mario left Camp Four one afternoon en route to the top of the world. Their plan was to ascend to the summit alpine style, using only what they could carry on their backs. Their first stop was Camp Five, which had already been established at 25,500 feet. We arranged for a radio call at 9 p.m. to monitor their progress.

At 9 o'clock, I called out on the radio for John McIsaac. There was no answer. I called again an hour later. Still no answer.

"It was a beautiful day," Denis recalls, "so clear and crisp, and we had such high expectations. It was sort of make Camp Five or bust and so I was very, very determined."

By nightfall, the weather had changed dramatically. The winds had increased to near gale force, hurling ice crystals across the ridge with the force of a sand blaster. The temperature, with the windchill, was pushing at least 40° below. The only way the trio could communicate was by huddling together with their backs to the wind and screaming at the top of their lungs. The roar of the wind was as loud as a jet engine. Making a radio call was impossible. Exposed fingers froze in seconds.

At 9 o'clock, I called out on the radio for John McIsaac. There was no answer. I called again an hour later. Still no answer.

My mind raced. Were they in trouble? Was John's radio dead? Were they dead? Everyone in Advance Base Camp became quiet.

At Camp Five, it was a different story. The wind was howling.

"I was quite frightened when we arrived at the scene of Camp Five and just the power of nature that was there,"

John recalls. "... I really felt like we were going to freeze to death."

Denis went ahead to locate the tent. The plan was to spend a short night in it and continue up the ridge the next morning.

"That was when I saw the remains of our tent," Denis recalls. "It had been torn and ripped and shredded by the wind... There were bits of tent fabric, and that was it. I remember falling down on it and feeling around to see what was going on, and there was no tent. No.

"I recall being absolutely devastated and thinking, 'Oh my God. This can't be possible.' I'd been saying to John and Mario all along, 'Look, we've got to get to that tent. We can get inside. We've got stuff there, we can carry on.' But there was nothing there."

Dejected, Denis descended through the raging wind to bring the news to his two companions in the darkness. He screamed in their ears: "There's nothing here!" Then he pointed up the ridge, made a flat motion with his hand as if to say the tent had been flattened and then he pointed down the ridge.

It was now about 10:30 p.m. The trio had been battling the blast for nine hours. The prospect of descending 2,000 feet back down to Camp Four was frightening. They were already shivering badly. They knew if they didn't start to move soon, they would be encased in ice. So, they started to descend.

"We got to a point where we said, 'This is crazy. We have to find shelter,'" Mario remembers.

Together, the trio tried to find a rock to protect themselves from the wind or a place to dig into the snow. It was all hard-packed ice. At one point, John sat down for a break. In a second, his sleeping bag was ripped from the top of his pack by the wind, blasted over the ridge and into the night. Before long, they were in trouble.

"We were all cold and shivering," John remembers. "There were times when we had to get down on all fours because the wind was so strong. We really felt it was going to pick us up.

"... The mission at hand became putting one foot in front of the other."

Mario went ahead to try to find the anchored ropes. Periodically, he would look back to ensure Denis and John were still moving. He hoped to get to Camp Four ahead of them and once there, prepare hot drinks for their arrival. Because Denis has a fear of descending alone and John is afraid of the dark, they moved behind Mario within 20 or 30 feet of each other.

Quickly, their Everest dream became a nightmare. The trio stumbled and staggered their way down, sometimes knocked over by the wind. At times, they feared they might be blown off the mountain.

"When I had left my two girls a couple of months earlier, I had promised them I would be back, I would be okay, that I wouldn't die on Mount Everest. And it was the thought of those two girls in my mind, two girls I love very much, that got me off Everest alive."
— John McIsaac

"Somewhere inside me, I found the strength to put one foot in front of the other," John recalls. "I thought of my two little girls, Leanne and Alicia. When I had left my two girls a couple of months earlier, I had promised them I would be back, I would be okay, that I wouldn't die on Mount Everest.

"And it was the thought of those two girls in my mind,

two girls I love very much, that got me off Everest alive. My two girls are young enough that I was able to use their age as a tool to put one foot in front of the other. I would recall walking six steps and taking a breath, panting for six breaths and saying to myself, okay, that's you, Leanne. I would then visualize Leanne's look as I left the airport. And then I would do the same for my daughter, Alicia, who is nine years old.

"It was that vision, that intensity of love, that got me off Everest. And to this day, I have a real appreciation for life."

Five hours after leaving their high point at 25,500 feet, the three would-be-summiteers arrived at the North Col. All they had to do was climb 30 or so yards to the safety of their tents. Unfortunately, it was all uphill.

"My legs were just shattered," John recalls. "You take one or two steps and rest... They were on fire they hurt so bad."

Finally, John and Denis lurched into Camp Four. Mario greeted them. They were weak and wasted, but fortunately, still alive.

"It was probably the coldest I have ever been in my life," Denis recalls.

Together, they survived the night. A makeshift sleeping bag was fashioned for John out of some equipment made of down. It was a long, cold night.

With sunrise came a realization. After seven years of work, "The Climb for Hope" was over.

Mario, John and Denis came down to Advance Base Camp the next day. At the bottom of the North Col slope, Mario turned and saluted Everest. Tears came to his eyes. He

> *"I think that in anything in life, if you give it everything you possibly can, you really do succeed."*
> — John McIsaac

The Power of Passion

knew everyone was safe, but he was so disappointed. Our time was over. He said thank you to Chomolungma.

Of four expeditions that made attempts on the north side that season, none made it to the top. The monsoon snows lasted too long and the winter winds started too early. The door to the summit never really opened. It slammed shut on us before we could even get a toe-hold across the threshold.

When we are faced with difficult moments in life, no one can give us the strength to continue. We must find it within ourselves, or ask that it be provided to us by a Higher Source, if that is what we believe.

"I walked away from the thing really knowing I did what I could," John recalls. "I think that in anything in life, if you give it everything you possibly can, you really do succeed."

"The mountain wasn't ready for us," Tim says. "The time wasn't right, or we weren't right..."

Disillusioned and disappointed, along with the rest of the team, Jamie and I descended to Base Camp.

"I remember struggling to get the lids back on our communications boxes," Jamie recalls. "It's one of the laws of travel that whatever you've packed into a suitcase on the way there magically expands during the course of your trip and will never go back into its container for the trip home.

"We also struggled to come to terms with the whole Everest ordeal, with our own feelings and with what others back home might say about our effort."

I remember how depressed I became. There had been so much build-up and now, it was over.

Coming back to Canada was the hardest part about that expedition. We were met by a hoard of reporters at the airport. They wanted to know why we hadn't made it to the top.

A few weeks after our return, I was introduced to an agent in Calgary who represents public speakers. "Oh," she said, "you were with the expedition that failed."

When we are faced with difficult moments in life, no one can give us the strength to continue. We must find it within ourselves, or ask that it be provided to us by a Higher Source, if that is what we believe. Jamie and I took comfort in the words of Mohandas Gandhi: "Full effort is full victory."

— JAMIE —

My position on the team was different from most of the others. I was the last to join. I paid for all my travel expenses and my role was to oversee the communications system with Al. For me, the trip was a grand adventure and a complete success. The day I left Advance Base Camp after Alan and I had argued about who would climb on, I already knew I would return to Everest. In fact, on my way down the East Rongbuk Glacier, I stopped to take a photograph with Everest in the background. I remember looking at the summit through the lens and then setting the self-timer so I could be in the shot. I knew then without a doubt that I would be back. I felt no sadness at leaving.

I knew then without a doubt that I would be back. I felt no sadness at leaving.

— ALAN —

Shortly after our return from Tibet, Jamie and I began to talk about how to get a permit to climb the mountain again. We were going back to Everest — together.

Re-Engineering the Dream

8

— JAMIE —

The return home from Everest was more than an emotional challenge. On a typical Everest expedition, you will lose 10 to 40 pounds — guaranteed. If you want to lose weight, go to Mount Everest. You don't even have to get out of your sleeping bag. Just lie there reading trashy novels and the weight will fall off. You spend so much of your time feeling weak and nauseous, eating is sometimes the furthest thing from your mind.

— ALAN —

It's the opposite when you come home. The most beautiful thing about coming home is you can eat totally guilt-free.

When I returned from Everest in 1991, I had lost about 15 pounds. We had a lay-over in Bangkok before our connecting flight home, so I left the airport and walked across the street to a nice, warm, well-lit restaurant. It's funny what you notice when you've been isolated for two months on a mountain. You have a whole new appreciation for things you never noticed before — like heating, electric lights, hot showers, water from a tap, physical touch and best of all for me — milkshakes.

I ordered the biggest chocolate shake they had. When the waiter brought it to me, I downed it in a minute. He was horrified. I immediately ordered another one, then another and finally, another. By the time I was done, I'd consumed close to a gallon of milkshake. I'm sure the waiter thought I was either a bulimic or a glutton. He'd obviously never served anyone fresh back from an Everest expedition. We're easy to pick out — we're gaunt, sun-burned, unshaven, and unkempt, but, can we ever pack the food away.

The easy part of the adjustment to western life ended in Bangkok. The most difficult challenge was adjusting to cultural time differences.

On Everest, time is almost meaningless. Monday is the same as Tuesday, which is the same as Wednesday. The only thing that changes is the weather. From timeless Tibet, where life goes on much the way it has for centuries, you are suddenly deposited by jet on a continent where time means everything — from newspaper and newscast deadlines for reporters who greet you at the airport, to de-briefings with sponsors, telephone messages, even bill payment deadlines.

> *Everest is more real than our world in the West. On Everest, if you make a mistake, you could die. In my eyes, that's as real as life gets — real consequences.*

For me, driving is the hardest. Everyone seems to be in such a hurry. My brother, Eric, welcomed me home to what he called "the real world." To me, Everest is more real than our world in the West. On Everest, if you make a mistake, you could die. In my eyes, that's as real as life gets — real consequences.

I returned to my apartment in Calgary where the Everest

dream had begun. There, Jamie and I began to ask ourselves a serious question. We had made our communications dream come true, but the expedition on which we'd been members hadn't climbed the mountain. Could we organize an entirely new expedition?

Jamie and I began looking seriously at the expedition's "failure" to determine how we might re-engineer a return to Everest. On a piece of paper, we came up with a list of 18 things we thought we might be able to do differently. This was a painful process. We had to put the past behind us, and come up with creative new ways to approach the Everest challenge.

We came up with some of the following:
1. No bottled oxygen
2. Fewer climbers
3. Less money
4. Different season

Most people think trying to climb Everest without oxygen isn't an improvement. To date, some 660 people have climbed Everest with the use of bottled oxygen. Only about 60 have done it without bottled oxygen.

Each oxygen tank weighs about 12 pounds. It lasts about eight hours. By the time you've purchased it, filled it, shipped it, insured it, paid customs duty on it, transported it to Base Camp by truck, carried it on the back of a yak to 21,000 feet and then had it carried on the back of either a Sherpa or a climber to about 25,000 feet to use it, each tank costs about $3,000 USD. On summit day, each climber needs two to four tanks. It is not uncommon for an expedition to spend as much as $60,000 USD on oxygen.

We decided to save our energies and money and go to the mountain with only emergency oxygen. Canadians had never climbed Everest without using bottled oxygen and we thought it would be fantastic to become the first Canadians to do it. Perhaps even Jamie and I might get the chance.

Next, we decided on a smaller team. Less climbers meant less equipment, food and cost. It would also mean less load carrying and a greater conservation of energy. So, we cut our team and budget to half what Peter's "Climb for Hope" had been in 1991.

We decided on a different season. The wet fall, post-monsoon season had produced terrible mudslides. We decided to go in the drier, spring season.

We also changed our marketing strategy. Instead of going after many small sponsors, we decided to go after one major sponsor.

This evaluation process, although difficult, was productive. Doing more with less has become a touchstone of modern living. Single parents do it. So do corporate employees and senior citizens. As prices rise and inflation continues, many workers have had their wages frozen, their salaries cut, or their raises sharply curtailed.

After making our changes on paper, we needed to take action. Our first step was to raise enough money to buy a permit to climb Everest. Jamie and I began to make new calls to see if we could create bookings for public speaking presentations about our 1991 Everest experience. We needed to raise $8,000 USD for the permit. Once we'd done that, we could go after a sponsor.

Doing more with less has become a touchstone of modern living. Single parents do it. So do corporate employees and senior citizens.

It was never a conscious decision to speak together. We just seemed to fall into it. I had made speaking presentations about my involvement in the 1988 Olympic Torch Relay and Jamie had experience as a broadcaster. We thought it would be fun to speak together. Everyone was talking about teamwork. We thought we might be able not only to talk about teamwork, but to demonstrate it.

Selling our idea to others wasn't easy. Again, we experienced a lot of rejection. No one knew who we were and our expedition had not made it to the top. Who would pay to hear a story about a team that hadn't summitted?

Our attempts to raise money for our permit through speaking took longer than we had hoped. So, I took a chunk of money from my savings and combined it with some money Jamie pulled in from his father, stepmother and grandparents. Together, we purchased our permit for the spring of 1994 from the Chinese Mountaineering Association in Beijing. Without a sponsor, it was an $8,000 USD risk, but we were driven to make our dream happen. Our financial commitment helped drive our personal passion.

To survive financially, Jamie was determined to sell speaking presentations. As usual, he pushed through almost any obstacle. One day, still suffering from the effects of diarrhea he probably contracted in Kathmandu while returning from the mountain, Jamie was on a conference call to a potential speaking client. He had three decision-makers on the line when he suddenly felt the need to answer a call of a different kind.

As he sat there on the phone, Jamie decided the deal was more important than his dignity. So, he closed the sale.

That incident demonstrated again Jamie's level of commitment to our Everest dream. With the 1991 expedition behind him, he was more motivated than ever. He said he needed the money to repay his grandparents and family for lending him the money to go to the mountain, but it was more than that.

Our first paid public speaking presentation together was to a group of sales people who worked for a Vancouver-based dairy. Excitedly, we boarded our first flight as paid business partners on April 9, 1992.

It did not take long for our enthusiasm to subside. Within minutes of being introduced, it became obvious our audience was drunk. Ten minutes into the presentation, a man in the front row vomited. Twenty minutes after that, a man at the back passed out and had to be carried from the room.

Jamie joked with this miserable group. I just wanted to get off the stage, leave all our precious slides and audio recordings, clothes and suitcases, jump into a taxi and fly home. I wanted nothing to do with professional speaking again.

Somehow, we finished the presentation. The client was happy, but we certainly weren't.

We laugh now, but then, it was devastating. Although the audience's reaction had little to do with us, like most presenters, we couldn't help but take it personally. I felt we had been mocked. Jamie was disappointed.

We overcame this setback the way we had learned to in the past. We got our eyes back on our goal. We focused on Everest. We needed money to pay our personal bills while we found a sponsor, and public speaking was our best way to do it. Over the next nine months, we poured ourselves into the challenge of creating speaking bookings. I also continued my freelance writing and together, Jamie and I scraped by.

We overcame this setback the way we had learned to in the past. We got our eyes back on our goal. We focused on Everest.

Then, on November 25, 1992, we got the break we needed. We were asked to a meeting with Mr. Alfred Balm, the chairman of a Calgary financial firm called "Emergo," part of the Luctor et Emergo (Latin for "I wrestle and emerge") Group of companies worldwide. This meeting was the culmination of a series of events five years in the making. First, I had spent four years writing *One Step Beyond*, a series of profiles of top adventure achievers. Second, after a former client read the book, he asked me if I would write a profile of Mr. Balm as part of an application for Mr. Balm to receive an honorary doctorate from the University of Calgary.

> As *a businessman, the challenges of taking risks, facing the unknown and achieving big dreams were second nature to him.*

In preparing the profile, I discovered Mr. Balm also had a passion for adventure. At one time, he had led a treasure-hunting expedition to South America. As a businessman, the challenges of taking risks, facing the unknown and achieving big dreams were second nature to him.

Mr. Balm was pleased with the profile I wrote on him. He surprised me one day when he called to ask if I would be interested in writing a book on the story of Emergo. I accepted and we arranged a meeting. Jamie and I saw our chance.

We met in Emergo's opulent offices on the 39th floor of a downtown Calgary office building. After briefly discussing the Emergo book, we moved on to other business. Our goal was to begin the lengthy and time-consuming sponsorship process with the introduction of the Everest idea. In successive meetings we hoped to lay out our climbing strategy, timelines, budget, and team make-up.

Our plan came off the rails five minutes later when I put an aerial photograph of Everest on the coffee table in front of Mr. Balm, a refined gentleman of Dutch origin. His eyes immediately lit up and he inquired:

"How much?"

"How much for what?" Jamie said.

"How much to sponsor your expedition?"

Believing this would be strictly a preliminary meeting, we had no budget prepared. In fact, aside from knowing the rough cost of the 1991 expedition, we had no specific idea whatsoever how much money we needed to go back to Everest.

Jamie backpedaled fast, explaining the costs in China were totally unpredictable.

Mr. Balm was not to be deflected. Sensing uncertainty, he leaned forward:

"Jamie," he said intensely, "how much?"

Jamie looked at me as if to say: "What the heck do we do now?" I looked back at him with a rapid raise of the eyebrow that I hoped would somehow communicate: "I haven't a clue, but for heaven's sake, we've got to say something."

After what seemed like an eternity, Jamie spat back a figure. It was not enough to fund the entire expedition, but enough for a serious head start.

"We're in!" Mr. Balm declared victoriously.

"You're in?" Jamie asked. "What do you mean, Mr. Balm? You wish to join our expedition?"

Mr. Balm leaned back in his plush office chair.

"No, Mr. Clarke," he said proudly. "We just bought your expedition."

As innocuously as possible, I tried to communicate non-verbally to Jamie to get the heck out of there. I didn't want Mr. Balm to have time to change his mind.

A few agonizingly long minutes later, the meeting adjourned. Jamie and I headed straight for the elevator, trying desperately to contain our enthusiasm. Nearly bursting with joy, we politely said our good-byes and pressed the "down" button for the elevator. It seemed like hours before it finally arrived.

We got in and just as the doors closed, we both let out a

The Power of Passion

victory whoop we're sure could have been heard through most of the building. We hugged and slapped one another on the back. Then we "high-fived." An otherwise ordinary elevator ride became a short victory tour. We had gone in with nothing but a dream, asked for what we wanted, and to our astonishment, received it.

> *We **had gone in** with nothing but a dream, asked for what we wanted, and to our astonishment, received it.*

As we skipped down the street outside, I flipped a $20 bill to a busker belting out opera on the sidewalk. Then we headed to a nearby restaurant to celebrate.

In retrospect, there was little luck in what happened that day. Five years of preparation, the resulting domino effect of several key relationships at just the right moment, and some good fortune culminated in a triumph. There was something almost kharmic about it — like it was meant to be.

We dubbed our expedition: "The Emergo Mt. Everest Expedition." Our slogan became "The Victory is in the Effort." We learned later that the choice of this slogan was one of the major reasons Emergo had agreed to sponsor the expedition, as well as our environmental philosophy of leaving the mountain cleaner than when we had arrived. Mr. Balm, it turned out, was one of the founders of the World Wildlife Fund.

In keeping with the climb's slogan, regardless of whether we made it to the summit, we wanted to come away from Everest with a sense of self-satisfaction, pride, and most importantly, knowledge that we could apply to whatever mountain we decided to climb next. It didn't matter whether that was a mountain of rock, snow and ice, a financial mountain, a health mountain, a business mountain, or a relationship mountain.

As Peter Austen and his team had done in 1991, we married our expedition with a charity. Because our goal was to climb Everest without bottled oxygen, we chose the Alberta Lung Association.

While I wrote the book on Emergo, Jamie hunkered down to begin organizing the expedition. His first challenge was negotiating the sponsorship contract with Emergo. This turned out to be an Everest in itself. It stretched on for months as half a dozen corporate lawyers acting on Emergo's behalf faced off against our only legal counsel, Jamie's older brother, Leigh, a lawyer, and Jamie, then 24. If Mr. Balm had done the negotiating, we mused, we would have had a contract in under five minutes.

The introduction of heavy legal fire power turned what otherwise might have been a straightforward partnership agreement into something more. Emergo's lawyers, who had been contracted from the outside, wanted to minimize their client's liability and financial risk — standard business practice. We wanted to stage the expedition. The worlds of adventure and law collided and Jamie and I began to learn some of the pitfalls of being "Adventrepreneurs."™

At one point, Jamie lost his cool. In a boardroom in Calgary, he found himself face to face with three lawyers whom together were probably earning close to $750 an hour.

He stood, put a well-worn boot up on a chair, picked up the 30-page draft of the sponsorship contract and said uncharacteristically:

> *I know I'm prepared to risk my life for what's on this pile of paper here.*

"I may not be a lawyer, but there's one thing I do know. I know I'm prepared to risk my life for what's on this pile of paper here. Whatever you may do to cover your own butts and that of your client isn't worth a hill of beans on Mount Everest. Until you're prepared to make the same commitment I'm prepared to make, don't talk to me about risk because you really don't know the meaning of the word."

Until you're prepared to make the same commitment I'm prepared to make, don't talk to me about risk because you really don't know the meaning of the word.

The boardroom went silent. After that, negotiations went more smoothly.

Eventually, the sponsorship contract was signed. Through Emergo's many holdings worldwide, we received outstanding administrative, organizational and emotional support. Indeed, the expedition became something of a corporate rallying point as organizations and personnel within Emergo's holdings that had previously not had a reason to interact suddenly did. Everest's influence, together with Mr. Balm's vision and decisiveness, positively affected the Emergo Group and the thousands of employees within it.

Jamie spent his non-negotiating hours on the phone, contacting suppliers and arranging for products and services for the expedition in return for benefits. In short, Jamie took care of many of the million and one nitty-gritty details that make an expedition. In our experience, people really start getting excited about an expedition three or four months before it departs, but by then, most of the work is done.

— JAMIE —

For me, there is a romantic charm in a project when it struggles along in its nascent stages. Fresh from your imagination, it is pure, unspoiled by reality, and unpolluted by the hands of the self-interested. This is also the most stressful time because it is steeped in uncertainty. This makes it both wonderful and hateful. Relentless effort is required to push through the paradox. In the end, it is only your belief and passion that fire the dream and blast it through the doubt and unfavorable odds.

While Alan wrote the Emergo book, I savored and cursed this time alone. The other team members worked on their respective areas, but Alan and I were responsible for raising the money, organizing the expedition and arranging logistics in Tibet. With Alan out of the loop temporarily, the organizational responsibilities fell to me. I enjoyed doing it alone. I felt it was important for Alan personally to write the Emergo book. Once we were on the mountain though, this decision added tension to our relationship.

The project's credibility increased dramatically once Emergo was involved. Investors often display what I think of as a herding instinct. The first major investor is always the most challenging to secure. But when other investors learn someone is backing a project, they are almost automatically interested because they don't want to be left out. Once you have the momentum moving in your direction, the money can begin to flow.

Fourteen hours a day, day after day, my time was consumed phoning around the world to secure equipment, arrange shipping to Tibet and liaise with the Chinese Ministry of Tourism in Beijing and Lhasa. I met with our sponsors and drummed up new ones. I worked with the other team members to attend to the thousands of details, each of which comprise a project of the magnitude and complexity of an Everest expedition. Through this period, I received incredible support from friends and family. They often brought me meals late at night, or simply accepted my absence from their lives. Looking back, I can barely comprehend where I found the energy.

In the middle of this organizational effort, I still had to

train physically. One night, my brother Leigh came along to run with me up the hundreds of stairs at the Canada Olympic Park ski jump in Calgary. It was well past 10 p.m. and a December ice fog had settled in the valley below. At the top of the ski jump tower, as we rested between intervals, we gazed silently out at the softened lights in the distance. I felt a tremendous calm settle over me. I had a sense of being in total control of the expedition responsibilities that rested on my shoulders. At first, it seemed like an inexplicable confidence, but I finally realized where part of the energy came from. Much of this momentum was created by the support of my brother, my family and my friends, even by the sponsors and the community members who believed in the project. I did not want to let them down. I wanted to assure them I was worthy of their support.

> I *felt a tremendous calm settle over me.* I *had a sense of being in total control of the expedition* responsibilities that rested on my shoulders.... Much of this momentum was created by the support of my brother, my family and my friends, even by the sponsors and the community members who believed in the project.

— ALAN —

The bulk of the work involved in climbing Everest involves raising money and then spending it wisely. At the time of this writing, the permit to climb Everest through Nepal costs $70,000 USD, including the bribes that are as much a part of doing business in this part of the world as tipping is in the West. Today's permit fee is almost 60 times the $1,200 USD price it was 15 years ago when Canadians first climbed Everest with the use of bottled oxygen in 1982. Fees continue to escalate.

The average commercially sponsored Everest expedition now costs $300,000 to $4 million USD and takes about three to seven years to finance and organize. Without a mountain of money, you cannot hope to climb the mountain itself, unless you are invited to join someone else's expedition. You probably wouldn't get that invitation unless you were a very strong high altitude climber. For us to climb Everest, we have to raise money. Fortunately, that is one of our strengths. We have to put a dress shoe in the business world to generate enough capital to put a climbing boot onto Everest. Eventually, we hope to be able to fund our own expeditions and branch out into other adventures — perhaps exploring the ocean depths, Antarctica and the Amazon. This has led to the development of our business niche, "adventure-entrepreneuring" or "Adventrepreneuring"™ as we call it.

Neither Jamie nor I pretend to be great climbers. We are not professional mountain guides who spend most of our lives in the mountains. We do not even climb every weekend. We spend more time climbing on and off aircraft to talk to groups about climbing the mountains of life than we spend climbing actual mountains ourselves. Despite a rigorous traveling schedule, however, we maintain a high fitness level.

Jamie and I leave the title of "veteran mountaineer" to the likes of Laurie Skreslet, the first Canadian to climb Mount Everest; Patrick Morrow, the second Canadian to climb Everest and the first person to climb the tallest summits on the seven continents; Sharon Wood, the first North American woman to climb Everest; Barry Blanchard, veteran of three Everest expeditions and Canada's leading alpinist, and Karl Nagy and Joe Josephson, two of the finest ice climbers in North America. There are many others.

Part of success in life is recognizing our strengths and weaknesses, not just in skills such as music and mathematics, but as human beings.

Part of success in life is recognizing our strengths and weaknesses, not just in skills such as music and mathematics, but as human beings. The routes Jamie and I have chosen on high altitude peaks have been largely non-technical in nature. They involve little hand- over-hand climbing on steep faces. Although we can climb steep ground when required, we prefer moderate routes we consider within our capabilities. We believe routes such as Everest's north and southeast ridges, which are steep hikes at extreme altitudes, to be within our abilities. We leave the extreme routes to more experienced climbers.

*   *   *

By the time I joined Jamie after finishing the Emergo book, thanks to him, the lion's share of the organizational work was well underway. There were still many critical details that had to be attended to, among them team clothing and climbing equipment such as tents, backpacks, sleeping pads and sleeping bags. I set about attending to them. While Jamie worked in an office supplied by one of the handful of companies Emergo owned locally, I continued to ring phones from my apartment. Although we were physically apart, we were united in the pursuit of our common goal. This time, we wanted to put the first Canadians on the top of Everest without using bottled oxygen. Perhaps we could be those Canadians. In 1991 our

Re-Engineering the Dream

role had primarily been to communicate, this time we wanted to climb.

In preparation for the expedition, we changed our training techniques. Rather than go into that dull, dingy and stinky stairwell, we made a suppliership arrangement with a downtown Calgary fitness club, Banker's Hall Club. There, we trained on inclined treadmills and pushed ourselves on mechanically-rotating sets of stairs. On weekends, we combined this with climbing in the mountains whenever we could, although our organizational duties did not allow us to do this with sufficient frequency.

As Pat Morrow, a member of our '91 expedition told us: "The best way to train for climbing is to climb." So, in January 1993, Jamie and I flew to South America as a two-man team. There, we climbed the tallest mountain in the Western Hemisphere, Mt. Aconcagua, in Argentina, 22,834 feet.

Our expedition to Aconcagua was a significant undertaking. As we already had commitments to our Everest sponsors, we felt a strong need to make it to the top. As a result, we brought enough food and equipment to last us well over a month. We knew that if our health and motivation held, even if there was as much as two weeks of bad weather, we still had enough food and supplies to make it to the summit and back down again.

Because of our strategy, Jamie and I shouldered 70-pound loads day after day. The other teams on the mountain, most of whose members carried 30 to 40-pound packs, called us "The House Humpers."

Things went well for us until just below our high camp at about 21,000 feet. Our plan had been to ascend the mountain's Polish Glacier and establish a camp just under a significant rock outcrop. We soon learned that with our heavy packs, we would not have enough time in the day to make it. So, we began to traverse to the mountain's regular

The Power of Passion

route to speed things up. The regular route was nothing more than a steep hike over loose rock. It was faster and safer.

On this traverse, at about 20,500 feet, I experienced one of my worst moments at high altitude. Exhausted from weeks of heavy load carrying and weak from the altitude, I sat down on a rock and honestly thought I might die there. I had a few Smarties left to eat, but I was so tired, I could barely get them to my mouth. Ahead of us lay a large snow slope I knew could take hours to cross. If the snow was deep and soft, it would be a terrible wallow. I wanted to quit. I wanted to let go of all the struggle and the strain and just sleep.

On this traverse... I experienced one of my worst moments at high altitude. Exhausted from weeks of heavy load carrying and weak from the altitude, I sat down on a rock and honestly thought I might die there.

Jamie took one look at me and one look at the snow slope. In an instant, he knew exactly what to do. Like a man possessed, he plowed through the snow, pounding out the steps with conviction. Halfway across, he hollered back at me, "Okay Al, she's all yours buddy. You can do this. We're getting out of here."

I dragged myself to my feet and set about following him. I was surprised how easy it was. That's because Jamie had done all the work. All the steps were packed down deeply into the snow. All I had to do was follow them. Eventually, we found a place to camp — in the lee of the howling wind behind a large rock.

The next day, we made our summit bid. It was an incredible experience. The weather was perfect — not a breath of wind and bright sunshine. We took the final steps

Re-Engineering the Dream

to the top together. There, we hugged. I cried. They were not tears of joy. They were tears of relief — relief that finally, all the mundane load carrying was over and there was no more up. It was just Jamie and me on top of the Western Hemisphere. It was wonderful.

Summit celebrations on high altitude peaks are rarely what many people imagine. You usually don't have enough energy to celebrate. That day, we did. It took us 90 minutes before we had all the summit photographs of sponsor banners we needed. Fortunately, the weather remained stable and we were rewarded with a stunning, 360-degree view of the Andes.

Once we had taken our photographs, we quickly descended to our high camp. An hour after we got back, the wind returned and the summit was ripped with fury. Mother Nature had perhaps thought us worthy. She had opened the door to the summit just long enough for safe passage. Then, she had slammed it shut behind us.

Days later, we reached the base of Aconcagua and began hiking out to the trailhead. The temperature was over 100 degrees Fahrenheit.

That hike was the most painful of our adventure lives together. The sun burned us. The air parched us. The rocky trail tore the soles of our feet to shreds. After two hours, Jamie had three-inch wide blisters on the bottom of both feet. He was forced to hobble for mile after excruciating mile. Finally, after 10 hours of agony, we arrived at the trailhead. There, we collapsed and sat in the sun like a couple of raisins. Jamie waved to passing cars like the Queen of England. We were drawn, besheveled and bearded, but we were victorious. We had made it to the summit and survived.

Choosing a High Performance Team 9

When we returned from South America, Jamie and I doubled our efforts to organize the Everest expedition. First, we had to choose our team. We knew who we wanted them to be. With everyone's technical climbing ability and experience at a high standard, we focused on compatibility first and experience second.

So often in life, especially in business, team members are chosen on the basis of experience first and compatibility second. A resume is a critical component in the screening process. We believe it should play a lesser role. Hard skills can be taught or acquired. Soft skills such as interpersonal abilities and equanimity cannot.

In a stressful situation, such as Everest can produce daily, it is not the hard skills that fail. When the wind is blowing, the tent is parting and you're tired, weak, sick and cold, human beings tend to direct their energies inward against each other, rather than outward toward the goal. Jamie and I call this kind of negative energy dissipation "auguring-in." On Everest, or in any life situation in which the stakes are high, once this downward spiral starts, it's difficult to stop. Many Everest expeditions dissolve in accusations and acrimony.

We didn't want that to happen with our team. So, we only invited climbers we knew well. In fact, we only chose those we knew from the '91 expedition. We didn't necessarily choose the strongest climbers. They were all strong. We chose the most compatible ones.

In addition to Jamie and me, our climbing team was comprised of four western climbers:

Dr. Denis Brown, of Fort St. James, British Columbia; John McIsaac, of Canmore, Alberta; Dr. Mario Bilodeau, of Chicoutimi, Quebec; and Tim Rippel, of Nelson, B.C.

We also had four Nepali Sherpas: Ang Passang Sherpa, Da Nuru Sherpa, Kami Tsering Sherpa, and Lhakpa Sonam Sherpa.

So often in life, especially in business, team members are chosen on the basis of experience first and compatibility second.... Hard skills can be taught or acquired. Soft skills such as interpersonal abilities and equanimity cannot.

Our support team was Michael Keller, of Calgary; Sarah (Sally) Wright, of Kluane, Yukon; Susan Foster, of Vancouver, B.C.; and Palde Tamang of Nepal.

Denis was a physician from a small town. John was a home builder. Mario was a university professor and Tim was a ski guide.

Our support team was no less eclectic. Michael was a teacher at a private school and Jamie's stepfather. Sally was the assistant Base Camp manager at a research station and Susan worked for an insurance brokers association.

To meld this diverse group of strong-willed, highly independent individuals into a cohesive team was not easy. Months before the expedition, we got the North American members of our expedition together to have a "bear pit session" on fear. We asked each team member: "What is your greatest fear about Everest?

> "... I'm not afraid to tell people I'm afraid of the dark. We all have fears."
> — John McIsaac

When you are alone at night, what do you wake up worrying about at 3 a.m.? What are you afraid to tell your friends, your children, your parents, even your partner?"

The responses were surprising. I spoke of my fear of the cold. Maybe it's because I have poor circulation, or low body fat, or a high metabolism. Whatever it is, on a mountain I can go from being fine to being almost unable to move in about five minutes. It happens most often when I am hungry and tired, but when it happens, it is terrifying. I shiver uncontrollably, my speech slurs, and I have a hard time performing even the simplest physical or mental tasks.

John McIsaac also had a revealing answer. He said he was afraid of the dark, especially the twilight and the unknown that would follow it. John is one of the most powerful high altitude climbers in Canada. He has faced many life and death situations in the mountains.

"One of my fears in life is getting stranded out at a remote place on technically challenging ground in darkness," John says. "It is one of my inbred fears. I take a headlamp with me wherever I go because of that.

"I don't know if it is something that happened in my youth in the dark or if it is something (about the fact) that I can't see, but I'm not in control of the situation... I find it extremely stressful operating in the dark, because if I don't have light, I can't move, and if I can't move, I'm stuck in the situation I'm in.

"... I'm not afraid to tell people I'm afraid of the dark. We

Choosing a High Performance Team

all have fears."

Each team member had a different prevailing fear. Denis said he was afraid of descending alone. Jamie said he was concerned about his climbing ability on technically challenging ground. Tim said he didn't want to leave his wife, Becky, a widow. Mario said he worried about his friends and family members back home.

Once some of our fears were out in the open, we asked each team member to identify how the rest of the team could help alleviate those fears.

I said the best thing they could do to keep me from getting cold was to watch me closely and ensure I ate something at least every hour. I had carefully researched and tested my clothing so I knew low blood sugar levels and fatigue were the primary reasons I became cold.

John suggested that if a team member knew they would be climbing with him into the dark, they could bring an extra battery for his headlamp and keep it warm in their suit. That way, when night approached, he could be assured he would have a bright headlamp to help him make it through the twilight.

Denis said that the best way to keep him from becoming anxious while descending was to stay with him so he knew he wasn't alone.

— JAMIE —

I've spent more than 20 years adventuring in the mountains, so I am secure with my ability to handle myself there from day to day. But because I was not as technically strong as the other climbers on the team, I was fearful I might hold the team back. I was concerned with how I might handle the situation if I was asked to lead a section of technical rock or ice at severe altitude.

In an effort to overcome this fear, I spent hours on moderate rock and ice routes in the Canadian Rockies, including solo climbs on the north face of Mount Assiniboine, the fifth highest peak in the range. It was rather tame by Rockies standards, but what Assiniboine offered was terrain similar to what we knew we would encounter on Everest's north face. On Assiniboine, I overcame my fear. I supplemented my solo climbing by getting out on the rocks with

Most people think high altitude mountaineering is a high risk endeavor. It is, but that risk, like most risks, can be managed.

my long-time friend, Aenea Palma. Aenea always "pushes his own envelope" and inspires me to push mine.

Once we got to Everest, I was totally comfortable with my ability and I was no longer fearful.

— ALAN —

All of us felt better after we had talked about our fears. By admitting our vulnerabilities, we became closer as a team.

At other team meetings, we continued re-engineering our expedition. We pulled out the computers and we planned, right down to the smallest detail, exactly everything we needed. Most people think high altitude mountaineering is a high risk endeavor. It is, but that risk, like most risks, can be managed. We manage that risk in the same way all businesses do — through careful planning, calculated risk-taking, hedging, crisis management planning, and the development of coping strategies.

We re-engineered a portable hydration system used by bicycle racers. It is called Camelbak. The Camelbaks consist of a long plastic bladder and drinking tube that sit comfortably in a pouch between your shoulder blades. Since the system had been designed for summer use, we had concerns the drinking tube might freeze on Everest. So, I asked my parents to test the tubing.

My father, Dr. John Peter Hobson (J.P.H. as we like to call him), a physicist, led "the experiment." He conducted a thorough test of the tubing, complete with freezing it in dry ice. He supplied Jamie and I with a written report of his findings. When it arrived, I chuckled. Here is an excerpt:

"FIELD TEST OF MODIFIED CAMELBAK SYSTEM: Jan. 1, 1994... (New Year's Day) A 25 lb. large packsack was loaded on the mountaineer (J.P.H.) and a walk of about 2 miles was undertaken in Terry Fox Park (in Ottawa). The toboggan hill was climbed. The drinking system was tested about every 300 metres (about 300 yards) and required opening the zipper of the ski jacket without gloves. Two mouthfuls were taken at each stop and spat out to prevent excessive urinating. The complete time for a drinking test (motion to motion) was 26 seconds, timed by I.M.H. (Isabel M. Hobson, my mother)."

My parents love me. Time and again, they have made these and other types of sacrifices for me. I count them among my closest friends.

While equipment was being tested, our expedition food coordinator, Sally Wright, was determining our dietary needs. At high altitudes, each climber requires 5,000 to 9,000 calories a day — double and quadruple the caloric demands of human beings at lower altitudes. Yet even with such a huge caloric intake, climbers still lose weight.

The reasons are many:

1. The lack of partial pressure of oxygen in the air means food does not fully digest. Many of the calories go right through climbers' bodies without being fully used.

2. The physical work of carrying loads on steep slopes is demanding.

3. The body's metabolic rate increases to adapt to the cold. Simply put, our fires burn hotter as it gets colder.

Sally spent countless hours alone in a warehouse in Calgary meticulously weighing thousands of pounds of food. She individually packed meals to streamline our movements on the mountain.

In the end, through teamwork and creativity, my individual weakness was turned into a team strength.

While this was going on, our team doctor, Dr. Denis Brown, was contacting the pharmaceutical representatives of dozens of drug companies to obtain a plethora of medications, antibiotics, antiseptics, intravenous drugs and other medical supplies to help maintain our health.

Specialized backpacks had to be manufactured. I chose a man I believe is one of the finest pack designers and manufacturers in North America. Through his tiny, two-person company, with two sewing machines stuffed into the back of a dusty warehouse, Larry Reid designed and built backpacks individually sized to each expedition member. Larry continues to design packs and other outdoor equipment for a company called Arc'Teryx in Vancouver, British Columbia. He is a quiet, humble man, but he has amazing technical and creative abilities.

Clothing was another critically important element. Because I get cold so easily, the team elected me to assume this responsibility. They thought, "Well, if Hobson can design clothing that keeps him warm, we'll all be toastie."

I worked with Calgary-based SunIce Ltd., a world-renowned ski wear manufacturer that had outfitted three previous Canadian Everest expeditions.

The process by which the clothing and other elements of warmth, such as sleeping bags, sleeping pads, mitts and hats was tested was anything but straightforward. We gained access to a cold chamber at the University of Calgary. There, for eight hours one night, Michael Keller sent me in and out of a wind-blown closet cooled to 25 degrees below zero. Within minutes of lying on the chamber's frigid stainless steel floor, I quickly determined how much of a company's success was marketing and advertising and how much was product performance. I concluded that the only real way to find out if something was as warm as the manufacturer claimed was to test it.

Every hour or so, I'd emerge from the chamber shivering and shaking, declaring between curses of vapor-curled breaths that, "This stuff sucks!" In the end, through teamwork and creativity, my individual weakness was turned into a team strength. On the mountain, I'd receive comments from fellow expedition members. "Hobson," they'd say. "What the hell's going on? It's 40 below and I'm sweating in this stuff. I'm trying to climb a mountain." It was "complaints" like these that made those hours of freezing my butt off worthwhile.

Toward the end of this intense two-year fund-raising, planning, and organizational process, Jamie and I became very tired. Jamie was working up to 16-hour days for weeks. When the time came for our expedition to depart, we were both exhausted. So, instead of working until the minute before our flight left for the mountain as I had done in 1991, I disappeared for 10 days of relaxation on Vancouver Island. Jamie flew off for some down time in Borneo. He wanted to visit the now famous Penan jungle people who inhabit the remote Sarawak rainforest.

In early February, our team convened in Bangkok airport en route to Kathmandu. With half the budget of the '91 trip, half the climbing team and no bottled oxygen, we had successfully re-engineered an expedition.

Now, we had to find out if we had the strength and determination to engineer a new outcome.

Facing Death 10

About the time Jamie was in Borneo and I was on
Vancouver Island, I learned that my nine-year-old nephew,
Michael, had developed bone marrow failure. His body
wasn't producing platelets, white or red blood cells.
Michael's older brother, Peter James, had died six years
earlier from the same genetic condition. He had been five at
the time. The whole terrible affair had begun innocently
when Peter had come home with a lump on his neck after
wrestling with some boys in the neighborhood. When the
lump didn't recede, doctors went to work. They determined
he had a rare, but advanced form of leukemia. At the time, I
was preparing to write the book on the Olympic Torch
Relay, *Share the Flame*. The project called for three months
on the road.

I last saw Peter James alive days before I left on the
relay. I tried to buoy his spirits by pushing him in his
wheelchair around and around the nursing station at British
Columbia Childrens' Hospital in Vancouver. We did about
five circuits, full out, running. The nurses gave us hell.

Peter James died five days before Christmas.

I remember calling my brother Daniel, Peter's father,
from the Torch Relay to begin arrangements to fly home for

Peter's funeral. Dan would have nothing of it. He said I should stay where I was, that I was making more of a positive contribution to the world with the Torch.

The trauma of Peter's death left Dan and his wife, Jane, badly shaken. Doctors said that because of genetics, there was a high chance Michael would develop symptoms of the same genetic condition. For years after Peter's death, a cloud had hung over Dan and Jane and to some extent, it always will.

When I got the news of Michael's diagnosis, I had an unsettling case of deja-vu. I was leaving on another trip and again, my nephew had been diagnosed with a serious illness. I was afraid lightning would strike twice in the same family and that I might never see Michael alive again.

Daniel, in his solid and courageous way, assured me Michael would be okay. He said Michael was much healthier than Peter had been, he was several years older and stronger.

> *There I was, off to climb some mountain, a risk for which Jamie and I had volunteered and prepared. Then there was Michael, stuck in a hospital bed as death stared him in the face. He hadn't volunteered for his mountain.*

Dan's comments were some reassurance, but Michael's situation gave me cause for serious reflection. There I was, off to climb some mountain, a risk for which Jamie and I had volunteered and prepared. Then there was Michael, stuck in a hospital bed as death stared him in the face. He hadn't volunteered for his mountain. On Everest, you can usually see what's coming at you. Michael couldn't. As a team of doctors took blood sample after blood sample, he began his fight for life. His battle included bouts of chemotherapy and radiation, debilitating procedures designed to kill the malfunctioning bone marrow. This produced nausea, vomiting and hair loss and made the discomforts we would experience on Everest look like a walk in the park.

If you want to see a hero, don't go to a mountain. Walk into your local children's hospital or cancer ward.

"They're bringing him as close to death as they dare," my father told me.

My mountain involved putting a flag into a patch of snow on the other side of the world. Michael's mountain really put things into perspective.

If you want to see a hero, don't go to a mountain. Walk into your local children's hospital or cancer ward. You'll see them, by the dozens and even hundreds. They are the patients, nurses, doctors, staff, families, and friends fighting a real uphill battle. They show the courage of heroes. When we climb mountains, we do it largely for ourselves. As the first person to climb Everest without bottled oxygen, Peter Habeler, of Austria, said: "Nobody's a hero who does it for himself... People who in life help others, they are heroes, anywhere in the world."

In my eyes, Dan and Jane are heroes. In 90 per cent of marriages in which a child dies, the marriage also experiences serious difficulty, including breakup. But Dan and Jane are made of strong stuff. They adapted to the death of Peter James by adopting a lovely baby girl, Taryn. With Michael's news, they were faced with the prospect of having to live their past nightmare over again. I couldn't imagine their anxiety and fear. Through them, and through Michael and Taryn, not through adventuring, I have come to know true courage.

On Dan's insistence, I flew to Nepal. I was anxious about Michael. It was some comfort knowing his doctors were far more qualified to help him than I was.

Our scaled down team of six North American climbers arrived in Kathmandu in February 1994 primed and ready. We were soon joined by our four Sherpas: Lhakpa Sonam, our sirdar, or head Sherpa; Da Nuru "Dawa" Sherpa, who had been with us in 1991; Kami Tsering Sherpa, a young upstart; and Ang Passang, a seasoned veteran. All had substantial experience on Everest. Some had been to the summit before. All told, we were half the size of our '91 climbing team.

In Kathmandu, we were also joined by our support team: Michael Keller, our communications coordinator and Base Camp manager; Susan Foster, our team manager; Sally Wright, our food coordinator; and Palde Tamang, our assistant cook.

The 10-day break Jamie and I had before our expedition was not long enough for us to even begin to recover from two years of the most intense effort we had ever made. A month or two was needed, but time was a luxury we didn't have. It was naive to assume we could bounce back quickly from the stress of dealing with suppliers, sponsors, shippers, customs agents and government officials.

Shortly after the team arrived in Kathmandu, likely as a result of fatigue from two intense years organizing the expedition, Jamie developed a sinus infection. Denis immediately started him on a course of antibiotics. Then, as we had done in '91, we loaded our two tons of equipment, half what we had in '91, into trucks and a bus and drove toward the Chinese border on "The Friendship Highway."

The highway was considerably friendlier this time. Because we had learned from our past and chosen the dry, spring season, we drove right by the spot of the landslides that had caused us so much grief in '91. When we got to the biggest former slide path, we pulled over and had a small celebration. It was a great moment. On the way to our goals in life, it's important to celebrate small victories. They help maintain our momentum, build confidence and keep us moving toward our objectives. If we only celebrate when we achieve our summits, we may be disappointed.

> *On the way to our goals in life, it's important to celebrate small victories. They help maintain our momentum, build confidence and keep us moving toward our objectives. If we only celebrate when we achieve our summits, we may be disappointed.*

Beside the road, we took a photograph to record the moment. In the background, we could see the debris left by the landslide three years earlier. Then, we hopped joyfully back into the bus and continued on our way.

Soon, we crossed into Chinese-occupied Tibet. Gradually, we began climbing onto the high Tibetan plateau above.

When we overcome one obstacle in life, we often encounter another. Instead of being delayed by mudslides, we now encountered snow. Because it was February, temperatures were colder. We groaned when we saw a huge snowslide blocking the narrow road as it hung precariously on the side of a deep stream valley.

Thankfully, we had anticipated this problem and already had a coping strategy. We pulled out our shovels and within three or four hours, we had dug our way through the worst of it. We celebrated again then. The way we saw it, our delay in '91 had been weeks. This time, it had been just a few hours.

Gradually, we drove up through the hills until the road spat out onto the arid plateau. There, the snow disappeared. We had entered the rainshadow of the Himalaya. We veritably flew across the plateau, waving to the scattered locals as we went. The only delay we experienced was in the tiny Tibetan village of Nylam at about 12,000 feet. There, Susan Foster, who lived at sea level in Vancouver, developed a sudden case of high altitude sickness. She had a terrible headache, was vomiting and was extremely weak. We put her into a portable high pressure chamber to simulate a drop in altitude and within hours, she was fine.

— JAMIE —

Everywhere we went in Tibet, we were met with curious glances, some slightly suspicious. People in this part of the world don't see many Westerners. There is no such thing as disposable diapers there either. Tibetans cut a hole in the seat of a baby's pants and the baby does its thing straight onto the ground. The team joked about what kind of tan line we might get if we tried wearing a pair of pants like that in North America.

— ALAN —

After a few more days of travel, we reached the ancient village of Xegar (JAY-GAR), just a day's travel from Base Camp. Here, near the site of that ancient monastery built on the top of a 16,000 foot peak, we took a few days rest in a run-down hotel.

For Jamie, the rest was uncomfortable. His sinus infection was not responding to antibiotics, and he said he felt like someone was blowing up a balloon inside his head. He was in a lot of discomfort, although in true Jamie style, he did not let on too much.

— JAMIE —

With a variety of bugs and spiders as my audience, I

tried to rest. Shiny, pearl-like fabric covered the damp, mildewing quilts that barely kept me warm. Although the hotel had plumbing, none of it worked. I was plagued with dysentery and the non-functioning toilets served only to tease me. I had to make the trip hourly to the outhouse outside. There, I gagged from the smell.

Once my arms began jerking against my will, fear set in. Unfortunately, I was unable to cry for help.

Even when I returned to my room, my memory triggered more gags. It was not a place to be sick.

Tired from all the work leading up to the expedition, my ability to hold off infection was greatly reduced. One infection took up residence in my nasal cavity. After oral antibiotics made no dent, Denis, our team physician and I decided to try intravenous antibiotics. As I despise needles, this was not a pleasant process, but Everest was worth it. Denis hooked me up.

After the first dose was administered, I was left alone to rest, but I soon started to feel odd. I had some trouble breathing and developed a case of the shakes as though I was cold. The more I tried to relax, the worse it became. At first, I thought I was having an anxiety attack because my breathing became erratic and I started to hyperventilate. I was more surprised than scared, but once my arms began jerking against my will, fear set in. Unfortunately, I was unable to cry for help.

A few minutes later, as though he had sensed my need, Alan walked in. In broken words, I asked for Denis.

"As soon as Alan told me Jamie wasn't breathing very well, I started running," Denis recalls. "When someone isn't breathing right on antibiotics, it means they're having something called an anaphylactic reaction... An anaphylactic reaction is the most serious situation that could ever be encountered by any physician. It is make or break. When someone comes in with a heart attack, you have some time to work. But an anaphylactic reaction is like an atomic bomb. It moves rapidly. People die within a minute.

"Usually, such a reaction happens in a hospital. If it had, I'd have been shouting and screaming for help, calling for extra nurses, getting one of the nurses to call for another doctor. And I'd have been calling for the crash cart in case he arrested.

"Jamie looked ashen and pale. He was sweating profusely, he was having difficulty breathing and he was retching. He just looked dreadful. His pulse was racing at a good 120 (normal for Jamie is about 50).

"I was thinking, 'Oh my God. Here I am in this dusty bowl, in this old, dry and dank smelly prison and there is nothing, nobody, that I can get to help me... I'm all alone'... I was terrified."

Denis's face telegraphed concern, but it never telegraphed terror. To me, he looked in control.

"We might need some oxygen soon," he said firmly.

I decided to stay and try to help in whatever way I could.

Moments later, Denis's tone changed:

"Alan — I need the oxygen — NOW!"

I tore out to the trucks and started frantically to search. As we hadn't planned on using our oxygen until we were on the mountain, no one knew where it was.

It was difficult for me to

move swiftly. We were already at 14,000 feet and I had not yet acclimatized. The Sherpas, who were standing outside the hotel, moved quickly to assist me. After rifling through our four trucks, all of which were packed to the rafters with equipment, we finally found one crate of oxygen tanks. Breathing heavily, I hauled it out from the bottom of the pile like an anchor. The crate was nailed shut.

Ten precious minutes passed. My mind raced with visions of Jamie suffocating. I tried to put them out of my mind and search for something to pry open the crate. Finally, Lhakpa produced a hammer from somewhere and we smashed the box to pieces. I yanked one of the cylinders from its berth, vaulted out of the back of the truck with it and ran to Jamie's room, breathless.

When I came through the door, Jamie's respiration was shallow. Denis snapped the tank from my hands, pulled out an oxygen mask and slapped it onto Jamie's face. Then, he produced a hypodermic needle, filled it with adrenaline and shoved it into Jamie's arm.

I went to Jamie's side and held his hand. I didn't know what else I could do. Susan lent her support too.

Jamie looked so pale. His eyes were wide open, but it was obvious he wasn't seeing anything. He looked terrified.

— JAMIE —

The room was electric with action. Out of character, Denis shouted orders. Tears welled up in Susan's eyes as she watched. Alan looked terrified.

Suddenly, it was as though the room had filled with water. Everything slowed. Sounds became muffled. In the eyes of the people who looked at me, I saw my fear. The only sound that was clear was my heartbeat. It was loud, but not regular.

I thought I might die. Cool tears streamed down my face. I became more sad than scared. Then, I was unable to breathe. The pauses between my heartbeats became longer. Slowly, I began to feel like I was falling into myself — slipping through the bed, past the floor and into the earth below. My peripheral vision started to fade.

In a panic, I screamed silently to myself, "No! I don't want to die!" For what felt like a minute, but which was perhaps only seven or eight seconds, my heart didn't beat at all. There was an intense silence — no noise or sound around me or in me. There, on an edge, I teetered. In that moment, I felt only deep sadness. But it was not born of regret. I had lived fully. I was comfortable with how I had lived my life to that point. My sadness came from the loss of life. I wanted to live more and be more with the people I knew. I felt unfinished in this world and not ready to go.

An injection of adrenaline from Denis brought an abrupt end to my descent. The room drained of water and thundering pounds in my chest awoke my heart and lungs. In an instant, I was among the group again.

> *Slowly, I began to feel like I was falling into myself — slipping through the bed, past the floor and into the earth below. In a panic, I screamed silently to myself, "No! I don't want to die!"*

— ALAN —

As soon as the adrenaline hit him, Jamie's respiration began to race. His chest heaved and his whole abdomen contracted violently. I was powerless and petrified. I just kept holding his hand and saying over and over again: "Hang on, buddy. Hang on."

He did. He always has. Jamie's never let me down and he didn't then.

The reaction passed.

"We did lots of talking," Denis remembers, "calming

The Power of Passion

him down, getting him to breathe slower, telling him to relax, telling him it was okay. That reassurance is very important."

Slowly, Jamie's color improved. His respiration returned to normal. After a few hours, Denis removed the oxygen mask.

> *That day in Xegar, life ceased being special to me and became precious.*

— JAMIE —

When the mask came off, relief marked the faces of the group, none so apparent as Denis's. I knew I was all right. In time, everyone left, except my stepfather, Michael. He crawled onto the bed and curled me up in his arms. Slowly, I floated off to sleep. His living energy flowed freely to me and I took it. This act of kindness was one of the most caring gestures another person has ever made for me.

Often since my experience, I have reflected on those moments of panic. Because of the encounter, I have become more comfortable with dying. I now know that when the time comes, I will slip down past my pain and into another world. I wonder if I will fight, or if I will know it is my time and simply go.

My view of life has changed. That day in Xegar, life ceased being special to me and became precious. Later in the climb, when John pushed for the summit, my decisions would be substantially affected by what had happened in Xegar.

— ALAN —

Mike held Jamie most of the night. The next day, Jamie was a lot better. By afternoon, he was his usual irrepressible self. He joked that the worst part of the experience had been the needle filled with adrenaline.

Denis's job wasn't finished. He got on our satellite telephone and arranged for Jamie to be examined at a clinic in Kathmandu staffed by Western doctors. Before going, however, we needed two more vehicles — one for Jamie, and another to take Susan Foster and me to Base Camp. We were still monitoring Susan to ensure she didn't have further challenges with the altitude. Like Jamie, I was also still tired from helping organize the expedition and had come down with a bad head cold. Denis said it would not be safe for me to ascend before my congestion cleared. At the air pressures of Base Camp and above, it can be difficult for even minor cuts to heal, let alone colds and sinus infections. They can quickly develop into more serious conditions.

In a bizarre turn of fate, in the dawn of the following day, Jamie and I stood in the parking lot of that dusty hotel in Tibet and watched bleary-eyed as our entire expedition, less us, left for Base Camp. I felt strangely detached from the scene, like I was watching it happen on some distant movie screen.

Two days later, after we had got the necessary vehicles and drivers, Jamie hopped into one truck, and Susan and I hopped into another. At the turnoff for Everest, we waved good-bye. A minute later, Jamie disappeared off onto the Tibetan plateau in a cloud of dust. Half of me went with him.

Communication Breakdown 11

Jamie was gone for 16 days. Meanwhile, the entire team worked liked fiends in Base Camp getting ready to move higher up the mountain. With Jamie gone temporarily, there was a leadership void. We still needed a point person to handle the big picture.

— JAMIE —

After my near fatal time in Xegar, I was saddened at not being part of the team when it arrived in Base Camp. As the organizational leader, I believed I had done my job well enough that the team would continue to function under Alan's logistical leadership, while John McIsaac marshaled the climbing resources. I believed that the project and the people had melded into a new entity and I was no longer essential to provide energy or direction. For me, this was a substantial accomplishment. For two years, we had worked alone in Calgary with only the germ of an idea. My separation from the team was the proof that the project was greater than my effort. I wished I had been returning to Kathmandu for a better reason, but I was at ease with my departure. I had no idea that the pressures of personality differences during the first days of acclimatization at Base

Camp would nearly ruin our years of work.

— ALAN —

Long before Jamie fell ill, it had been agreed that Susan Foster was to lead the team from North America to Base Camp. Once in Base Camp, Michael Keller was to lead us to Advance Base Camp and from there, John McIsaac was to lead us up the mountain. That is what we had planned, but that is not exactly what happened.

The team approached me to fill the leadership void created by Jamie's absence. Having busted my tail with Jamie for two years, raised close to $500,000 to finance the expedition, struggled financially and worked horrendously long hours to make the dream a reality, I was loathe to jump quickly from the role of expedition organizer to expedition leader, even if only temporarily. I had read many accounts of Everest expeditions and I knew expedition leaders rarely made it to the summit. Their energies were usually used up directing the team's movements.

In assuming we could pass the torch to other team members, Jamie and I made a major mistake. That mistake cost our friendship more than all the mistakes we had made to that point added together.

As one of the main reasons for helping stage the expedition was to see how high I could climb, I was not interested in leading the team, nor did I consider myself qualified. My concern was that if I moved into the leadership role now, even if only for a few days, I might never be able to remove myself from that role later.

In reality, by organizing the expedition with Jamie, I was

already in a leadership role. I now realize I could have no more removed myself from that role than Jamie could have. In assuming we could pass the torch to other team members, Jamie and I made a major mistake. That mistake cost our friendship more than all the mistakes we had made to that point added together. And it continues to adversely affect our relationship today.

My desire not to fill the leadership void caused frustration and confusion in the team. They countered by putting pressure on me to re-assume the role I had played in 1991 as communications coordinator. I also refused to take on those responsibilities, for the same reasons I had declined becoming expedition leader. Like everyone on the team, I did my best to help where I could, but I deliberately resisted any attempt to pigeon hole me into a support position. In my mind, my role was clear — as had been agreed, once I had helped get the expedition to the airport, I was now to be a climber. Unfortunately, I don't think the team saw me that way. They saw me as the expedition co-organizer/leader and wanted me to continue in that role.

— JAMIE —

On March 8, 1994, I passed the Rongbuk Monastery with high expectations for the team, a pack full of goodies from Kathmandu, a case of beer, and a set of small audio speakers on which to play music in the kitchen tent. When I arrived in Camp, I received a warm reception from the team. Then I set about talking with individual members to get a sense of where we were. It didn't take me long to realize that much of the team's delight was generated by their need for someone to assume leadership over the expedition logistics — a vacuum I had not anticipated.

I sensed considerable frustration with Alan's reluctance to assume the organizational leadership role. I too was surprised by Alan's decision and bewildered when we discussed it. It was clear to me and the rest of the team that our mission was to put the first Canadians on the summit without the use of bottled oxygen. Even our press kit and subsequent press releases mentioned this ambitious goal. I believed we had long ago abandoned the idea of discovering how high we could go individually as the primary purpose of the expedition.

Having assumed a commitment to our sponsors and the team members we had invited to join the expedition, our single mission had become, as a team, to reach the top. It seemed logical that Alan could best help ensure this outcome by continuing in an organizational role in my absence. No one expected him to be the climbing leader. John McIsaac would handle that.

First, I was angry, then disappointed, then resentful. I could not believe my partner was unwilling to do what was needed to help make the climb successful. I couldn't help but think of the situation we had faced in 1991 when Alan and I had decided who would climb on and who would descend to operate the communications system. To this day I have not been able to come to terms with Al's leadership decision.

Of course, the leadership issue was not the only area of conflict within the team. Like most Everest expeditions, we wrestled with personality differences and the common realization that our teammates had their shortcomings. Most surprisingly, our Sherpas managed to destroy my own mythology of them when I came upon three of them in a literal three-way brawl, triggered apparently by personal tensions that surfaced under the pressure of our expedition.

These issues only tend to highlight the fact that a considerable part of the struggle on the mountain is interpersonal. Everest is a pressure cooker that forces us into rigorous self-examination. Part of Everest's magic rests in the painful reality we find inside us. Everest exposes things about ourselves we often successfully hide at more reasonable altitudes. The rapid pace of an expedition leaves little time to attend to our character flaws. We don't have the necessary energy anyway. The larger question is ultimately, will we hide from our new self-knowledge, or will we change and grow from it? Most searingly difficult experiences are like this. They are characterized by pain and loss, achievement and gain. The only guarantee of failure comes from our refusal to grow from our new self knowledge.

Everest is a pressure cooker that forces us into rigorous self-examination. Part of Everest's magic rests in the painful reality we find inside us. Everest exposes things about ourselves we often successfully hide at more reasonable altitudes.

In the immediate term, I set about making some changes on the team. The first plan was a team party. It seemed to help morale. The team had already been in Base Camp for more than two weeks and it showed. I felt as though I had failed them not being there and so I doubled my efforts to repair things as best I could. The group refocused at this point, not due to my efforts really, but because we had a mountain to climb. A level of professionalism was re-established. Climb is what we did.

Alan saw my move back into the leadership role as an error. I knew that it was both ethically and practically the right thing to do. We had responsibilities to our sponsors — to Mr. Balm, whom I felt had made an investment not just in the idea of climbing Everest, but in me personally. The best way for me to live up to this was to put someone on the summit. Even though I could clearly see Alan's position, this was not the Alan and Jamie show. True, we had done the largest share of the work and the thought of watching someone else stand on top, I must admit, left me with a feeling of envy. The reality was that Alan and I knew we would not be the strongest of the climbers. Our responsibility, I felt, was to the team and to our sponsors. I have found a lesson here for myself though, and I am saddened that it comes at such a cost. I have learned to be more accepting of other people's motivations. In the past, I have been too zealous in imposing my ideas on others. Alan was free to do as he pleased. He did not need to be berated by me for what I thought was right. In hindsight, I would not change my decision to accept leadership. On the other hand, I would have changed my judgment of Alan's actions. I was too hard on him. I should have left him to struggle with his own journey in his own way.

— ALAN —

My position not to jump into the leadership void, for which I was accused of being selfish, had far-reaching effects on my relationship with Jamie. When he eventually returned to Base Camp in improved but not complete health, any uneasiness between myself and the team then subsided to a large degree, but it grew between Jamie and me. Jamie's behavior was consistent — others first, Jamie second. Unfortunately, my behavior was also consistent — my goal first.

Jamie and I never clearly communicated the reasons for

> *I would have changed my judgment of Alan's actions. I was too hard on him. I should have left him to struggle with his own journey in his own way.*

The Power of Passion

our respective decisions until much later in the expedition. By then, irreparable damage had been done to our friendship. For weeks, we silently resented each other. I resented him for what I thought was a foolish waste of his already depleted energy reserves. I felt he should save his remaining energy for climbing the mountain and let Michael and John take over team leadership as had been agreed. Jamie resented me for what he thought was self-serving behavior.

Once trust is lost in any relationship, it is like a mirror struck by a stone. Although all the tiny pieces can be glued back into position, the mirror always shows the cracks.

In Jamie's view, our goal was to put the first Canadians on the top of Everest without the use of bottled oxygen. I understood that, if possible, it was also to put either him and/or me on top. This fundamental misalignment of goals, which should have been worked out months before the expedition, somehow got lost in the myriad of organizational details and only surfaced on the mountain. Amazingly, it was a fundamental decision we overlooked and a major mistake. By the time we came face to face with it, it was too late. The depth and quality of our friendship took a serious nose dive and it has never been, and probably never will be, the same. Jamie claimed I was self-centered. I said he was unclear of the goal and lacked focus. Both positions had merit, but somewhere in the middle fell out the most important element in any relationship — trust.

Once trust is lost in any relationship, it is like a mirror struck by a stone. The glass shatters. Although all the tiny pieces can be glued back into position, the mirror always shows the cracks. They are deep and numerous.

That's what happened to Jamie and me in 1994 and we both regret what happened. A stone did hit our mirror and we have been struggling to re-glue the pieces ever since. When you run any relationship through not just one, but two Everest expeditions (and a third approaches), it's a bit like putting beef through a meat grinder. What comes out the other end is dramatically different from what went in. Change is part of relationships, as it is part of life.

I take full ownership of my decisions during these two incidents — my decision to climb higher in '91 and my decision not to step into the leadership void in '94. I also accept responsibility for the subsequent effect it had on my relationship with Jamie. If I had been more flexible, perhaps these mistakes could have been avoided.

One of my greatest strengths is my ability to focus on a goal. When I do, I can lose sight of others. Our greatest strength can also be our greatest weakness.

If I had to live my life over again, I would not change my decisions. I'm not sure Jamie would either. I have to be true to myself, as Jamie does to himself. We differ fundamentally on some issues, we all do as human beings. Jamie and I also see the world from much the same viewpoint on other issues. For me, the victory is that we are still able to work together. In our view, a team doesn't always have to get along. There can be differences within a team. In fact, Jamie and I believe it's impossible to have a true team without differences. Our differences make us stronger — provided they do not destroy our relationships.

One of my greatest strengths is my ability to focus on a goal. When I do, I can lose sight of others. Our greatest strength can also be our greatest weakness.

For me, Everest is all about

my relationship with myself. It's about coming to terms with myself and what I perceive to be my past failures. If I cannot have a good relationship with myself, I cannot hope to have a good relationship with Jamie or with anyone else. I believe, perhaps mistakenly, that getting to the top of Everest some day may help improve my relationship with myself. I hope it will give

> *It's **impossible to have a true team** without differences. Our differences make us stronger — provided they do not destroy our relationships.*

me the satisfaction of knowing I accomplished the most difficult physical thing I could imagine. But as someone once said, "A man who is incomplete without the summit cannot hope to be complete with it." As imperfect human beings, I believe we are all incomplete to some degree. I am keenly aware of my incompleteness, as I am of my weaknesses and strengths. As a colleague of mine recently pointed out, "Everest is a great goal, Alan, but what happens if you don't make it to the summit? You have your pyramid firmly planted on its point."

The relationship rift that resulted from the '94 communication breakdown between me and Jamie has been the greatest loss in my Everest experience to date. It also ranks as one of the greatest losses of my life. Expeditions come and go. Barring an earthquake or World War III, Everest will always be there. But friends like Jamie come along once in a lifetime.

As the leadership and goal misalignment issues continued to fester in our relationship, Jamie and I shifted our focus to climbing the mountain. We got the communications system running. This was a victory. In '91, a single box containing our satellite telephone and support equipment weighed about 250 pounds. Now, three years later, thanks to advancements in technology, it weighed 48 pounds. The entire satellite telephone came in a briefcase. The cost per minute to use it however, had risen to about $18 USD, instead of the $12.50 USD it had been in '91.

"Satellite phones are like lingerie," Jamie says. "The smaller they get, the more expensive they get."

After spending about two weeks in Base Camp getting acclimatized, the team began a series of acclimatization hikes designed to introduce our bodies to higher altitudes. I wasn't even able to complete these mild altitude gains. I was too weak. It was disheartening and embarrassing to have to admit that in spite of all my training, my body was simply not adapting as quickly as that of the other team members. I had come down with the flu and although I tried to remind myself of my nephew Michael, and his strength, I became disheartened. If I felt this badly now, how was I ever going to climb higher?

"Alan, this is no time to look ahead," my mother said firmly but supportively over the satellite telephone one day. "One step at a time. Just hang in... your energy will come back."

> *On Everest... you may as well be naked. Everyone can see your weaknesses and strengths. The strain of high altitude lays your emotions, motivations and character bare.*

On Everest, as Jamie has said, you may as well be naked. Everyone can see your weaknesses and strengths. The strain of high altitude lays your emotions, motivations and character bare. The intense physical exertion makes you particularly vulnerable emotionally. Tears come easily. So do feelings of joy. Everest is a place of emotional peaks and valleys. You can't hide behind office walls, job titles, salaries, cars or neighborhoods. Nor can you easily go home. You must face yourself. Because of this, Everest appeals to Jamie and me. It's about as fair as we think the world gets. The mountain is completely indifferent to a person's age, nationality, income, material wealth, race, or even language. On Everest, we are exactly who we are — warts and all. We call her "The Great Equalizer."

On the advice of my parents, I hung in. Soon, a team of yaks arrived to transport our gear to Advance Base Camp at 21,500 feet. As usual, they amazed us with their feats of strength, agility and endurance moving huge loads up 4,000 feet over rough terrain. They came with yak herders and Jamie's friends from '91 were among them.

From Base Camp, as Jamie and I have said, Everest looks indescribably huge. It scrapes the sky, silencing your soul. We never use the word conquer in association with Everest or in association with any other mountain. Everest cannot be conquered any more than nature can. It has its rules and laws and we must live by them. The mountain's forces are so powerful it can extinguish life as easily as we blow out a candle. The only conquest is one over our own weaknesses and fears. The real mountain is inside us. The journey is inward.

Sir Edmund Hillary perhaps said it best: "Mount Everest is never conquered. Occasionally, it tolerates a momentary success."

With the help of the yaks and yak herders, we established Advance Base Camp about a week later. There, we were treated with a sobering view of the deadly North Col slope, that cemetery in the snow for some 70 or so other climbers.

Because we had chosen the spring season instead of the fall as we had in '91, we established our next highest camp on top of the North Col comparatively quickly. Our Sherpas were essential in this effort. They worked tirelessly ferrying loads up and down the slope between Advance Base Camp and Camp Four, a vertical gain of more than 2,000 feet. While the rest of us took six to eight hours to make the round trip, they did it in half the time with double the weight.

The wind on top of the Col was often gale force. Some nights, you could lie in your tent and feel the wind struggling to lift you off the snow. We used fish netting over some tents to keep them from being blown away. At times, the roar of the wind was so deafening it was like trying to sleep inside a jet engine. Jamie and I wore earplugs, but they didn't help much. I tried to forget where we were and reassure myself that the tent was firmly anchored.

Camp Four is one of the few places in the world where you must never sleep walk. Ten feet outside the front and back of your tent are 2,000-foot drops. Going to the bathroom there can be life-threatening. How do you go to the bathroom at 40° below? The answer is quickly. Believe us, it adds a whole new meaning to the phrase, "freezing your butt off"!

Every few weeks, I'd call my nephew Michael to see how he was doing on his mountain. After he had survived the chemo and radiation therapy, doctors had proceeded with a bone marrow transplant. With our communications system, I could call him from anywhere on Everest right to his hospital bed. He said very little, but he is a fellow of few words even when he is well.

Michael amazed me with his courage. He seemed singularly unabashed by the whole bone marrow thing, but instead appeared resigned to taking one day at a time and leaving the worrying to Dan, Jane, Taryn and the medical team. Like Jamie, his biggest concern seemed to be his fear of needles.

"To a small boy, a needle is more dominant than other

aspects of life," my mother told me.

Like I had with Peter, I tried my best to raise Michael's spirits. Mostly, I just told him I loved him and described some of the challenges we were facing on Everest. I hoped he could relate. Dan said he was thrilled to get the calls as I'm sure any nine-year-old would be. I was disappointed he had to receive them in hospital. Unlike his late brother, however, at least he was alive to receive them. I was grateful for that.

Michael amazed me with his courage. He *seemed singularly unabashed by the whole bone marrow thing, but instead appeared resigned to taking one day at a time.*

I remember hanging up from those calls and thinking that despite our challenges, we were lucky to be alive. We hadn't been relegated to a hospital bed by some cruel genetic twist. We were living our dreams.

By early April, Michael's body had begun manufacturing new white blood cells, an optimistic sign that the bone marrow transplant was starting to work. Before month's end, he had been discharged from hospital. Jane's sister Mary, arranged for him to be chauffeured home in a stretch limousine. There, Dan, Jane and Taryn received him with balloons, hugs and lots of kisses.

As Jamie and I looked up at Everest, Michael raised our spirits. Everest was a big and dangerous mountain, but compared to Michael's, our summit seemed a lot more attainable.

Rising to the Challenge of Change

12

We changed our climbing strategy in '94. In '91, our plan was to climb Everest's north ridge to the point it intersected the northeast ridge. Then, we would follow the northeast ridge for over a mile to the summit, climbing a series of three rock steps along the way.

The problem with the '91 route was the long traverse to the summit. It took place entirely in "The Death Zone," the area above 26,000 feet that will only support life for short periods of time, usually only a day or two. In The Death Zone, every step can be excruciatingly difficult. The partial pressure of oxygen plummets to about one-third what it is at sea level and suddenly, the line between life and death can become as delicate as the strand of a spider's web. Here, the slightest puff of bad weather hits climbers hard and can quickly extinguish life. In such a place, what might be regarded as only a minor squall at lower altitudes can become a ferocious storm.

In '94, for safety reasons, we decided to make our traverse of the mountain lower, below The Death Zone. Our plan was to climb the north ridge to about 24,500 feet, then make a hard right and traverse the eastern half of the north face to the middle of the face. There, we would establish

Camp Five at the base of The Great Couloir or Great Gully, a huge feature that clefts the north face in half. We would then work up the couloir and establish Camp Six at just over 26,000 feet. From this camp, we could launch our summit bid by climbing a rockband and onto the summit pyramid above.

Our plan went smoothly, to a point. We ascended the north ridge, turned right, crossed the face and established Camp Five at about 25,000 feet. Our Sherpas helped make this possible. As a stabbing wind ripped across Everest at about 50 miles per hour bringing with it windchills in the triple digits, they moved load after load into position by climbing face first into the blast. In one Herculean push, they allowed our expedition to make a quantum leap closer to the summit. When they returned exhausted to Advance Base Camp, we "fêted" them like returning champions.

John, Denis and Tim then took over. They pushed up the couloir and in only a few days, put in Camp Six just below the rockband.

Our expedition was now within 3,000 feet of the summit. We were just a day and a half from triumphantly planting the flag on the summit and realizing our dream. It was not to be that easy. At a time when Everest normally gets only the odd dusting of snow, it began to snow heavily. Three days later, it was still snowing. By sunset, about a foot had fallen since midnight. Coupled with similar snowfalls the preceding two days, the combined accumulation turned the north face into a huge avalanche slope. For any mountaineer, there could not have been a worse place to be than in the middle of the towering 10,000-foot-high wall.

Unfortunately, that's exactly where Mario Bilodeau and Lhakpa Sonam Sherpa were — and had been for three days.

"If the snow doesn't stop soon, we could be in trouble," Mario said over the radio from his perch with Lhakpa in Camp Five. "I don't get a good feeling about this."

"Hold your position," replied John from Advance Base Camp. "If you move now, you could trigger a huge slide. There's about 4,000 feet of fresh snow loaded on the slope above you. We don't have much of an option but to wait it out."

"Roger," replied Mario, his voice telegraphing concern, "but if we don't get a break soon, we won't be able to fix the rockband."

The growing avalanche hazard was only part of our team's obstacles. A 300-foot high rockband of near-vertical climbing stood between us and the summit. It was the last major geographical obstacle challenge separating us from our goal.

It had taken two months of back-breaking work to establish Camps Five and Six. As they lay in their tent, Mario and Lhakpa knew that with every passing day, the rarefied air was making them weaker. The cells in their bodies were not getting enough oxygen to regenerate.

It had taken two months of back-breaking work to establish Camps Five and Six. As they lay in their tent, Mario and Lhakpa knew that with every passing day, the rarefied air was making them weaker. The cells in their bodies were not getting enough oxygen to regenerate. The dry mountain air was turning their respiratory tracts to coarse sandpaper. Just rolling over in their sleeping bags made them pant.

But they couldn't move. It wasn't safe. Besides, their mission was incomplete. They had to anchor rope through the rockband and in so doing, open the door to the summit for the team's strongest climbers. Once the rockband was fixed, three years of intense organizational effort could culminate in victory. Without rope through the rockband, nothing could happen.

Chomolungma was not in the mood to cooperate. Irritated perhaps by our flagrant invasion of her privacy, Everest refused to give ground. For two more days, the snow continued. By Thursday evening, four days after it had started, about four feet blanketed the north face. It began to slide through the door of Mario and Lhakpa's tent.

"If you want to reach the summit of Everest, you have to take some chances sometimes," Mario recalls. "You don't want to abandon right away. You have to go as hard as you can before you abandon. If the snow stopped and the conditions got good, we were in a good position to go higher."

The snow didn't stop. During a radio call that evening, the team debated what to do. Everyone agreed avalanche conditions were extreme. There was less agreement on what to do. Finally, it was decided to wait until 6:30 a.m. the next morning to make a decision.

To compound their problems, Mario and Lhakpa had very little fuel left for their stoves. If they ran out, they would have no way to melt snow for water. Without water, they could dehydrate and die. They were caught in the ultimate Catch-22 — if they descended or if they stayed, they could die.

"Lhakpa prayed most of that night," Mario remembers. "I prayed also. He told me, 'I'm praying, Mario, but I'm not praying only for us to make it down. I'm praying for our souls'... I knew what he meant, but I didn't want to discuss it."

That night, another foot of snow fell. The pair lay wide-eyed in their tent as avalanche after avalanche poured down the face. The slides sounded like freight trains. As Mario listened, he thought about his late brother, Jocelyn, and his deceased father, Real. Their memories were a source of great comfort. They helped him get in touch with what was important — life.

At 3 a.m., tired of the torment, Lhakpa rolled over:

"He said 'Let's go down. Let's go down, go down, go down,'" Mario recalls.

Sherpas have a close spiritual connection to the Himalayas. It is their home. They have a sound decision-making ability, one based on years of experience combined with intuition. When a Sherpa says it's time to go down, it's time to go down.

Sherpas have a close spiritual connection to the Himalayas.... When a Sherpa says it's time to go down, it's time to go down.

Together, Mario and Lhakpa decided not to call the rest of the team to let us know they were leaving Camp Five. They also decided not to call at 6:30 a.m. either. They knew the American team on the North Col would see them traversing and would relay the news they had left Camp Five.

"We knew the rest of the team would tell us not to go down," Mario remembers. "There was nothing they could do for us anyway. We wanted to concentrate on nothing else but trying to make it through. We would call when we were safe."

At 4 a.m., in the dark, Mario and Lhakpa crawled out of their tent in Camp Five, turned on their headlamps and looked around at the north face of Everest. Below them was a 6,000-foot sheer drop. Above them was 4,000 feet of heavily loaded avalanche slope. One misplaced step and they would vanish into the night. For safety, they had to move at night when the mountain was coldest and least prone to avalanches.

Everyone on the team knew it wasn't just the snow conditions that made their situation dangerous. Lhakpa wasn't carrying an avalanche transceiver — a beacon that would allow him to be located if he were caught in a slide. None of the Sherpas wore them. They believed that if it was their time to die, nothing could save them. We knew that if Lhakpa wasn't wearing a transceiver, he would have no way to locate Mario if he were trapped in a slide either. They would have to rely on a combined 40 years of mountaineering experience, luck, and their physical and spiritual strength if they were to make it safely back to Camp Four.

"Before we started, I tested the snow with my ice ax," Mario says. "It was very fragile... I could cut it with my hand...we decided to go anyway."

Before they set out, in a moment of silence, they prayed again and threw rice as an offering to the gods. Then, they took their first tentative steps into the unknown.

Their first challenge was a large snow slope. Even by the light of his headlamp, the sight of it sent Mario's heart racing.

> *They would have to rely on a combined 40 years of mountaineering experience, luck, and their physical and spiritual strength if they were to make it safely back to Camp Four.*

"I thought, 'Oh, my God. If that goes, I will go for sure.' If you fell, you were gone."

Not far below them was a cliff several hundred feet high. Days before, the leader of an Italian expedition had fallen to his death here.

In the middle of the slope was a steeply angled rock covered with snow. Mario thought that if they could just get there, they would be safer.

From Camp Five to the north ridge, expedition members had anchored rope. In normal conditions, Mario and Lhakpa would have clipped themselves into this rope and followed it across to the ridge, about a mile away. If they had fallen, the rope would have held them.

These were not normal conditions. The rope was now buried under snow. If they tried to extricate it in the wrong place, they risked cutting the top layer of snow. This could cause a slide. Mario and Lhakpa didn't dare tie themselves together with their own rope either. In these unsettled snow conditions, if one of them fell, he might take the other one with him.

These were not normal conditions. The rope was now buried under snow. If they tried to extricate it in the wrong place, they risked cutting the top layer of snow. This could cause a slide.

Gingerly, Mario took his first steps toward the rock. It was hard work. He was thigh-deep and wallowing. Fortunately, the snow seemed surprisingly stable. In minutes, he reached the outcrop. Lhakpa joined him a few minutes later. He took over the lead. Because the snow was less deep where he was, Lhakpa clipped into the anchored rope.

The snow slid.

"Lhakpa lost control," Mario remembers. "I thought he was gone."

In a second, the slide tore part of the rope from its anchor. It swept Lhakpa, still attached, toward the cliff below. For a second, the Sherpa thrashed for purchase, spinning as he went. Then suddenly, it was over. Within inches of the edge, the rope went taut. The snow poured over the precipice in a torrent.

Both men struggled to catch their breath. After they had recovered emotionally, they continued their traverse. There was no time for delay. In hours, the sun would rise and heat the face, causing innumerable avalanches. If they were to survive, they needed to get to the north ridge as soon as possible.

Thankfully, the traverse to the other side of the snowslope went well. By first light, they had reached their second major challenge — a steep snow chute, or couloir, heavily loaded.

"It was at that point that I was probably the most scared," says Mario. "I looked at the couloir and said, 'Uh oh.' I didn't feel good about the couloir at all. I looked at it and I said, 'Oh shit.'"

Quickly, they evaluated the situation. There was an ethereal aura to the place, a stillness. Mario told Lhakpa to unclip from the rope and wait at the side of the chute. His intuition told him Lhakpa's spiritual strength would be more important than the rope's strength. As Lhakpa repeated a mantra in hushed tones, Mario felt a peace come over him.

"I had more confidence in his mental state, watching me and praying than trying to hold me (on the rope) if something happened. If there was a slide, I knew it would be impossible to save me."
— Mario Bilodeau

"I felt good about Lhakpa. I felt really strong about the man and his philosophy, about his strength, and not just his physical strength, but mainly about his spiritual strength...

"I had more confidence in his mental state, watching me and praying than trying to hold me (on the rope) if something happened. If there was a slide, I knew it would be impossible to save me. So, I started into the couloir on the rope."

Mario tried to take big steps

to prevent creating an unbroken line of footprints that might trigger a slide. He moved like a soldier through a mine field — a carefully placed foot here, another there.

There was a sudden "whoosh" sound. Mario dropped a few inches deeper into the snow as an air pocket beneath the snow collapsed under him.

"I thought, 'God. It's going to fracture somewhere.'"

It did.

Slowly, the snow beneath Mario's boots started to move. Instantly, he took a few quick steps forward toward the next anchor. But then, the snow above him started to move too. A second later, cracks appeared in the snow all around him.

"Lhakpa screamed: 'Mario! Mario! Avalanche!'

"I turned around and right away I screamed back: 'Lift the rope! Lift the rope!'"

Like a bantam weight lifter displaying superhuman power, Lhakpa yanked the rope over his head in one continuous motion. The avalanche went under it.

Mario was knocked on his side, but the rope held his fall.

Then, as quickly as it had started, the avalanche stopped.

"... Everything was completely peaceful," Mario remembers. "You couldn't hear a sound.

"My heartbeat was probably over 200 (normal is about 70) from the exertion of the altitude, the exertion of moving through the deep snow and from the stress... It was then that I realized we were really in big trouble. We were really in big shit.

"'Then, I thought, I've got to make it across.'"

Desperate, but thinking only of survival, Mario lengthened his stride. If he was going to die, he resigned to himself, he wasn't going to die waiting for the bullet. He was going to die fighting. With everything he had, Mario Bilodeau began to march. In the space of about 50 feet, he entered a whole new dimension of commitment.

"Then, from exhaustion, I was not able to pull the rope from under the snow anymore. I couldn't. I tried and tried and tried."

Strung out in the rarefied air, heart, lungs and adrenaline racing, Mario reached the end of his energies. With just 40 feet to go to the side of the couloir, he hung like a rag over his ice ax.

After many minutes of panting, he came to a realization. In the middle of one of the most dangerous places in the world, he knew he would have to unclip from the rope and solo his last steps.

"I was really scared. I looked down and I saw a piece of rock coming out of the snow. I told myself, 'If I fall, if there's an avalanche, I have to hit that rock and hopefully, it will stop me.'"

It was wishful thinking. The reality was that in his state, if anything untoward happened, he was gone. His legs burned and his arms were limp.

He settled on a compromise. As he couldn't lift the rope from the snow, he tied a short length of cord to it from his harness. After he had assured himself it would slide along with him as he moved, he collected his thoughts and tried to renew his resolve. Like a drunk man, he staggered forward. About five feet from safety, he could not drag the cord along the rope anymore, so he unclipped from the rope. In a combination of bold defiance and resignation, on the count of three, he dove towards the side of the couloir and swung his ice ax into the snow.

It planted with a reassuring

> *In the middle of one of the most dangerous places in the world, he knew he would have to unclip from the rope and solo his last steps.*

"thud."

For a moment, he just hung there, gasping, unable to move. Then, like a man coming back from the dead, he hauled his limp body out of that icy grave and onto the rock above. For the moment, he was safe.

Many minutes passed before he could do anything but breathe. When he regained his composure, he looked back at Lhakpa. He was only about 100 feet from him, but it seemed like a mile.

"ABC to Mario and Lhakpa...." There was no reply. In Advance Base Camp, we listened as avalanche after avalanche poured down the north face.

Lhakpa elected to mimic Mario's closing charge. With the benefit of knowing Mario had made it, he veritably flew across the couloir. He hauled the rope out of the snow with conviction and soon, he joined Mario on the other side. Together, they hugged.

While this drama was unfolding, a smaller one was happening below. At Advance Base Camp, we scoured the north ridge with binoculars, searching for signs of the pair. There were none.

John picked up the radio. "ABC to Mario and Lhakpa...
"ABC to Mario and Lhakpa..."
There was no reply.

In Advance Base Camp, we listened as avalanche after avalanche poured down the north face. Swirls of snow swept over the north ridge in sinister sweeping motions, curling their frozen tongues over the edge like some beast licking its lips. Swirl after swirl circled overhead. Then silence... absolute silence.

"Try again," Jamie said.

"ABC to Mario and Lhakpa. ABC to Mario and Lhakpa.

Come in Mario and Lhakpa. Come in."

Silence.

It is hard to describe the feeling you get when you begin to realize that two people, two people you have laughed with, struggled with, fought with, cried with, two people who have joined you in one of the most intense efforts human beings can share, may forever have vanished from your life. The finality of it all is hard to comprehend — how one minute they are talking to you vibrantly on a radio and the next, the only sound that comes back is the wind. It is a solitude that transcends human experience. You feel like you are falling and falling through space. Then, you hit bottom, and the pain comes — like someone is eviscerating you with a hot poker.

Because of the locations of Advance Base Camp and Camp Five, Mario and Lhakpa were in a radio blackout area. Even if they had had their radio on, we would not have been able to reach them. We could only watch and wait. Advance Base Camp became deathly quiet.

> *It is hard to describe the feeling you get when you begin to realize that two people you have laughed with, struggled with…may forever have vanished from your life.*

When Mario and Lhakpa crawled out of that couloir, they crawled back into our lives. The balance of the traverse to the north ridge was dangerous, but not as treacherous as what they had already been through. They fell a few more times from exhaustion and from slipping on the snow-covered rock, but again the rope saved them. There were a few more close calls, but nothing on the scale of the near-catastrophe in the couloir.

The Power of Passion

About 2 p.m., 11 hours after starting out, their boots finally touched the solid rock of the north ridge. They arrived together.

"We looked at each other, we looked back at what we had done, we hugged and we stayed there at least 15 minutes," Mario remembers. "We just sat there. We didn't say anything. We just thanked God we had made it."

Moments later, the silence in Advance Base Camp was broken. A halting, hoarse, but breathing voice crackled weakly on the radio.

"Mario to ABC."

John snapped his radio to his mouth.

"Roger Mario. This is John in ABC. Go ahead Mario. Go ahead."

"It's Mario and Lhakpa from the ridge. We made it."

We have never celebrated the sound of a voice like we did at that moment. Only seconds earlier the team had begun to enter the depths of despair. Instantly, agony became ecstasy. We jumped and cheered and jumped again, laughing and crying and laughing again.

Mario and Lhakpa safely descended the ridge to Camp 4 and from there, continued down the North Col slope to Advance Base Camp. There, they were welcomed like heroes, given food, drink and warm congratulations. In no time though, they had retreated to their tents to sleep.

Lhakpa disappeared within himself for three or four days after that. He prayed in his tent and only appeared for brief moments. Mario ate, drank and talked about their experience. He also talked about going home to go fly fishing. Incredibly, in a few days, his strength returned and he began talking again about another summit attempt. Mario has incredible resiliency.

"I think Lhakpa's reaction (to our experience) was more spiritual than mine," Mario remembers. "I prayed a lot too. I was very close to my soul and very close to my father and

Rising to the Challenge of Change   135

brother. Something was very special."

En route from Camp Five to Camp Four, Mario and Lhakpa survived six slides, two of which almost swept them off the face. But with the relief they were still alive came the realization that Camps Five and Six had been swept down the face. Fortunately, the camps had not been occupied at the time, but in one, 30-second-long avalanche, two months of work was eradicated. The situation was both joyous and sad.

— JAMIE —

We were now faced with a pretty substantial challenge, but our choice was simple. We either continued to go for it, or we left.

Al and I hadn't worked at this for two years and struggled away on the mountain with the rest of our team to turn around now, beaten by the weather again like we had been in '91. Most of us felt our effort had not yet been total.

> *Al and I hadn't worked at this for two years and struggled away on the mountain with the rest of our team to turn around now, beaten by the weather again like we had been in '91. Most of us felt our effort had not yet been total.*

So, we began to strategize. We came up with a plan to take another route on the mountain, a route that was being climbed by an American team. It was the same route we had tried in 1991. Now though, instead of attempting it with bottled oxygen as we had then, we would try it without. It was either that or leave.

We decided to keep climbing. After negotiating with the American expedition, we received permission to share their route. Gathering together what little equipment we had left, we headed back up Everest. In return for carrying more oxygen higher up the mountain for the Americans, we were given use of some of the tents they had already established there. This combined with some of the sleeping bags and stoves we had left, gave us just enough gear for a summit attempt.

Our plan was to break our team into three waves of two climbers. At this point, our Sherpas had given it everything they had. When your Sherpas are spent, that's always a sign things are getting tough.

— ALAN —

It is usually obvious who the summit teams are — they are the strongest and healthiest climbers. Sometimes, they are the only climbers left standing. Throughout the expedition, John, Tim, Denis and Mario had been climbing particularly well. At a team meeting, we agreed John and Tim should go first. But, as usual, Everest had her say. Tim, unfortunately, fell sick climbing up toward Camp 5 and Denis decided he was well enough to go in Tim's place.

"Each of our waves of two climbers would be a day apart," Jamie recalls. "The first team would go for the summit. If they had any problems, there would be two other teams behind them to help. If the first team made it to the top, great, they would drop down and the second team could go for it. If they didn't make it, the third team would try. Using this leap-frog technique, we might have as many as three shots at the summit three days in a row, if the weather held."

On May 22, as the wind tore at our tent in the team's new Camp Five on the north ridge at 25,500 feet, Jamie and I realized we had reached the limits of our energies. This was as high as we could go. From here, the team's stronger climbers would carry the torch.

Thanks to Mario and Lhakpa, we all had an example to follow.

The Power of Passion

The Power of Love 13

On May 25, 1994, at about 4 a.m., our two strongest climbers, John McIsaac and Denis Brown, left American Camp Six at just over 26,000 feet on Everest's north ridge. Because the return trip to the summit can sometimes take as long as 24 hours, it is critically important climbers start early, or risk having to descend, exhausted, in the dark.

Camp Six was a wind-swept hell hole. It was steep and sloping and all of the tents were pitched on an uncomfortable angle. The ground was so steep climbers moved between tents along anchored ropes. Combined with the altitude and the elements, it was an unpleasant place.

Denis was especially tired. He had not slept in three nights and had eaten little.

"I cannot sleep in tiny tents with somebody else," he says. "I get very claustrophobic... I had been propped up on my elbows, trying to breathe. I have to be able to see out of the tent. I had almost thought of turning back and going down because I couldn't get enough sleep... When we got to Camp Six, I was really tired."

John and Denis spent an uncomfortable night in Camp Six. They had planned to leave at midnight, but by the time they got their boots on and had melted snow to fill their

139

water bottles, it was 4 a.m.

As John and Denis climbed out of their tent, their headlamps stabbed into the darkness. Their bulky clothes made them feel like stuffed penguins. Beneath them, peaks we had looked up at for months were now at their feet. Clouds snaked through the valleys below.

"I had a whole lot more confidence than I did in '91 simply because I had a bit more experience behind me and things felt really good," John recalls. "I felt strong, I felt keen and I felt very aware of what I was doing... I was just on a real psychological high with the fact we were really starting to make tracks. I was really trying to bring out what I felt inside... The summit looked so close, it really seemed feasible that we could stand up there. I used to dream about what I would do on the final steps getting to the summit. I still do. You have to envision what's going to happen because that is part of the psychological game that drives the physical body."

Together, the pair became lost in the "two foot wide" world illuminated by their headlamps. It took some time before their bodies began moving smoothly. Gradually, their breathing, although rapid and labored, became rhythmic. Anticipation and excitement overrode anxiety.

> *"You have to envision what's going to happen because that is part of the psychological game that drives the physical body."*
> — John McIsaac

In no time, John was ahead of Denis. He moved strongly toward the northeast ridge and two hours later, the pair climbed into the dawn. The Himalayas exploded in light. A shadow of the summit cast down upon the top of the clouds.

"The day looked good," John recalls. "There was beautiful sun on the summit. I feel more comfortable when it is light as opposed to dark. As soon as it became light out, there was an energy that was placed in me. It really felt good. I thought we were going to stand on the summit."

Denis was about 300 feet below John. He was already beginning to feel tired and cold. Without bottled oxygen, as difficult as it is to breathe at these altitudes, it can be just as difficult to stay warm. The blood is not only the agent for transporting oxygen to the tissues. It also carries life-preserving heat, especially to the extremities.

Once they got to the ridge, their first obstacle was a 100 foot high outcrop called "The First Step." The first of three such rock steps on the ridge, this one was draped with pieces of old climbing rope left behind by previous expeditions. At sea level, the step would have been a breeze to climb. But here, at about 27,000 feet, as Denis lumbered along in heavy clothes and mitts, goggles and thick boots, it was dramatically more difficult. One mistake at the wrong moment and you could fall 8,000 feet down the north face.

"I saw John go over it (the first step) solo," Denis recalls. "I looked at the thing and I was just horrified. I thought it was going to be easy, but it was steep and sheer and there was all this horrible snow all around."

Slowly, Denis started up the step. He got about 25 feet above the ridge and suddenly, the ice and snow collapsed under his feet. His heart went into his mouth. Thankfully, he only slid back down to his starting point, arriving at the bottom in a lump. He had somehow missed falling down the face.

"That step was bad news," Denis remembers. "Then I turned around and looked at the view and thought, hey, this is great. Maybe I could turn around here. It wouldn't be too bad. I've tried and I've slid down. But then I thought, nah, come on. It was early in the morning and I thought I could give it another go."

He did. He pulled on the old rope and panting and puffing and grunting, somehow, he got up. The summit was still quite far away. By now, it was about 10 a.m., the time when many climbers like to be within a short distance of the top.

Denis looked around him. The wind was howling up the far side of the mountain, sending clouds swirling viciously over the ridge and with them, spin-drifting snow. It was freezing cold — at least 40° below. Through the gale, he peered up the ridge in search of John.

"I remember thinking, 'I know John's worried about me, but he's also got his own objectives'... It was okay, we had an understanding."

At these altitudes, there is only enough energy for yourself. Any attempt at rescue can prove fatal not only to the climber being rescued, but to the rescuer as well. John and Denis knew this. They were each responsible for their own safety.

Mechanically, Denis began to plod up the ridge.

"But I was losing control and I hate losing control. I was stiff, very stiff and tired and very cold."

As he moved further up the ridge, Denis could feel himself getting more and more tired. His pace slowed to a crawl. From his medical training, he knew he was on the verge of hypothermia, a condition in which the body's inner temperature begins to drop. If it falls more than a few degrees, death can be imminent.

> At these altitudes, there is only enough energy for yourself.... John and Denis knew this. They were each responsible for their own safety.

"I lost all feeling in my feet and hands," he recalls, "but I was getting cold inside, and that began to worry me. And so about a quarter of the way along the ridge, I stopped and sat down."

In retrospect, there was perhaps nothing worse he could have done at that moment. Less movement meant less body heat and less body heat meant a higher susceptibility to hypothermia. He was too tired to care. He couldn't even eat or drink. It took too much effort. His altimeter read over 28,000 feet — still 1,000 feet from the top.

Then a strange peace came over him.

"The summit was up there, not that far away... But then I turned around and looked at the view again. It was very, very comforting... It was very peaceful. I could see the earth curving away and I thought, 'You know, this is not bad. It's okay. I'm all right.' And I was at peace with myself. I wasn't disappointed at all."

At 11 a.m., after battling for seven hours, Denis Brown reached his high point on Everest. He sat there in the snow for 30 minutes just looking at the view. Then, knowing he was being seduced into perpetual sleep by the cold and inactivity, he pushed himself up from the ridge and began to head down.

The descent was horrible. When he got to the top of The First Step, he just lowered himself down the ropes and prayed they would hold. They did. When he reached the ridge below, he continued his slog towards Camp Six. In the back of his mind, he wondered what sort of state John would be in if he came down.

Shortly after noon, exhausted, Denis arrived safely at Camp Six. He zipped open the tent, and crawled straight into his sleeping bag. After a few hours, he warmed up, dozed off and awoke a short while later. Then he turned his attention to making hot drinks and having something to eat.

While Denis's summit bid had ended, a drama of a different sort was beginning above him. John had reached "The Second Step," a malignant block of rock with a 20-foot aluminum ladder swinging precariously in the wind from it. The ladder had been placed there many years before by another expedition to make the ascent of the step easier.

Like Denis, John had now begun to get tired.

"You take four or five steps and then you'd huff and puff for maybe 20 breaths and then do it again," he recalls. "... I'd have to stop and pant like hell."

Despite the exertion, John remained optimistic about his summit chances. Although the weather had deteriorated, he wasn't frightened. He'd heard lots of stories about the weather suddenly changing up high and people dying of exposure. He tried to stay in tune with what was happening inside him and around him.

Slowly, he climbed up through a narrow opening in the rock, then traversed a small snow slope that led to the ladder. Since John makes his living building houses, he was comfortable on ladders. This one was different. Over the years, some of the lashings that had been used to anchor the top of it to the mountain had fallen off, leaving its top rungs free to sway more and more over the 100-foot sheer drop below. Beneath that was the huge north face and the Main Rongbuk Glacier below. As the wind blew, it shook the ladder, causing the top of it to bend like a tree top over oblivion. He prayed it would hold.

Everest moved at his feet — back and forth, back and forth, with each new frigid gust. He clung to the thing, his life literally suspended in space.

"The thing starts swaying, and the wind starts blowing and it's blowing the snow down from above and your goggles are all frosted up. You're in a hell of a predicament. You want to keep going, but all of a sudden, the wind is shaking this ladder."

Desperate to hang on, John

The Power of Passion

hooked an arm through a rung and prayed. Everest moved at his feet — back and forth, back and forth, with each new frigid gust. He clung to the thing, his life literally suspended in space.

Eventually, between gusts, John was able to inch upwards — one shaky rung at a time. He finally made it to the top of the ladder, adrenaline coursing through his veins. He could hear his blood pounding in his ears.

From the top rung, panting uncontrollably, he reached for a piece of tattered rope. Somehow, it held. He hauled himself to the top of the step.

That's when reality hit. As a blast of ice crystals struck him full in the face, he realized The Second Step had taken him one step closer to extreme exhaustion. Unknown to him, his lungs were silently beginning to fill with water, a condition called pulmonary edema.

John was now faced with an agonizing decision. Could he make it to the top? He was within 750 feet of the summit. The question that bothered him more was, did he have the strength to make it back?

"That is where the drama really played itself out," he recalls. "It was quite a struggle and an emotional roller coaster. Every once in a while, the clouds would open up and I could see the summit. It really looked close."

Most climbers who die on Everest die on summit day, retracing their steps. Sometimes, their ambition exceeds their energy or ability. The lure of that patch of snow is so powerful, so magnetic, that they are drawn toward it as if by some unseen force. If they are fortunate enough to reach the top, their summit fever can suddenly break, catching them unaware. They can then find themselves instantly exhausted, staggering down the mountain. As they try desperately to cling to life, they can collapse, stumble and fall, or simply sit down in the snow for a nap and never wake up. The Mother Goddess takes them in her arms and sweeps their spirits away.

We feared that might happen to John.

"You fantasize about getting to the top," he says. "You fantasize about being the first Canadian to do it without bottled oxygen. I was trying everything in the book to keep me going. It seemed I was coming close to what was going to be the margin I needed to get back to Camp Six. It is one thing to climb the mountain. It is another to get back."

As if in slow motion, John squeezed out the painful steps, one after another, after another. In the lee of the wind behind some boulders, he took shelter just below The Third Step.

From below, we monitored John's progress through binoculars and spoke to him on his radio. His wife, Cathy-Anne, was in Base Camp. She also offered encouragement. That human contact helped him feel less alone.

But he was done. None of us, not even Denis, could possibly have climbed up to help him. So, someone, or something else, did. It delivered a message.

"I am not a Christian or anything, but I think there was a point where someone was saying something to me, saying, 'You have crossed the line and you are not coming back'... It wasn't something I could hear like a voice in me. It was more of a subtle feeling that in this zone and at this time, between here and that third step, I could go to the summit, but I wouldn't come back."

> "It is one thing to climb the mountain. It is another to get back."
> — John McIsaac

For an hour, John was tormented at the top of the world. He started forward a few steps, then stopped. Then he began to descend, but stopped again.

"No!" he told himself. "I can't quit. I have to try harder."

Another 20 or 30 feet up, then sit in the snow. Evaluate. Wrestle with himself. Get up, wrestle with the mountain. Which was worse?

"We cheered him on," Jamie remembers, "but when he reported fatigue and cold setting into his core, I considered the late hour and encouraged him to descend. John must have felt very alone up there."

Then, John reached the end.

"I just broke down and cried. I had to take my gloves off and put my hands over my eyelids because they froze shut. As soon as I got the ice off my eyes, I looked down the ridge towards Camp Six and I realized the decision was made...

"That really hurt... I was truly wasted."

At 3 p.m. on May 25, 1994, just 521 vertical feet from the top of the world, John McIsaac reached his physical summit. Given the thin air, he might have been able to hit the top with a stone from where he was. It was a horizontal distance of less than two city blocks. Most people could have walked it in a few minutes at sea level. But, of course, he wasn't at sea level.

"John was still certainly lucid," Jamie remembers, "but we didn't know how much energy he had left. We knew he needed encouragement, some kind of contact with the world beyond the mountain. So, we fired up the communications system and patched a call to Canada and the national TV studios of the Canadian Broadcasting Corporation. We got a reporter on the line."

From his seat at 28,500 feet, one of the world's highest viewpoints, John looked out over the Himalayas. With the summit in sight, he struggled not only to answer the reporter's questions, but to breathe. As we listened, John announced his decision to a nation:

"Well, Blair, (breath) I can see it (the summit) and it beckons me (breath, breath)," he told the reporter. "... and I go on for 20 (breath) more feet (breath, breath) and I rest for 15 minutes (breath) and I try (breath, breath, breath) and go on more (breath). But I know (breath) it's just too far (breath, breath). I feel (breath), I feel fatigued (breath), disappointed (breath, breath), relieved, I guess (breath, breath), I can't go up any more (breath, breath), without ah (breath), jeopardizing my life (breath, breath, breath).

"I've accepted that (breath, breath), I (breath), I ah (breath, breath), I don't have it in me (breath, breath), not this time (breath), not the sequence that took place (breath), ah, (breath), to make it to the top (breath, breath), over."

— JAMIE —

In what was a sound mountaineering judgment, and what I see as a moment of personal greatness and strength, John made the decision to descend — to turn his back on the top. I supported his decision. I had suggested descent and my suggestion was what he needed to hear. I think he was grateful for what little support I did give him.

Several days before, I had carried oxygen to Camp Five. After the eight-hour carry, I was spent. Just below Camp Five, I began coughing up blood. I knew then that I would not be able to safely go any higher... Regardless, I should have been in Camp Six as support for John's push. I felt like I was on Earth and he was on the moon.

> *In what was a sound mountaineering judgment, and what I see as a moment of personal greatness and strength, John made the decision to descend.*

— ALAN —

In my tiny tent in Camp 5, as I listened to the interview, tears began to stream down my face. I wrote in my diary that night:
"Heart-wrenching

disappointment... That it should come to this after three years of work — alone, cold, wind howling. A bridge too far."

There, panting, John looked out into the beyond. He thought about '91. He thought about that terrible descent in the dark. He also thought about Cathy-Anne. And, he thought about his two daughters.

He needed to talk to them — now. He needed to hear their voices. He needed something to hold on to besides mangy bits of rotten rope or the thread of his own wavering will. If he was to make it back, he needed a reason to come home.

"I just let them know I couldn't make it and that I was turning back. 'We love you, Daddy,' they said. 'Please come home.'" It would be a long walk.

At his request, we used the satellite phone for its most important call. Half a world away, at 3:30 a.m. their time, Jamie got John's two daughters, Alicia and Leanne, out of bed.

"I was in tears," John remembers. "I told them where I was and that I had cried. I told them it was a selfish thing to do, but I also needed to hear their voices to keep me going. I apologized that I couldn't make it. I just let them know I couldn't make it and that I was turning back."

"We love you, Daddy," they said. "Please come home."

It would be a long walk.

Slowly, John dragged himself from the snow and began his descent. Periodically, he lost his footing and stumbled forward. Then, the image of his two daughters played in his mind. Their words struck his core in a way deeper than the wind and cold did. Together, they grabbed him by his climbing suit, pulled him to his feet and nudged him gently onward.

"We love you, Daddy," they whispered again in his head. "Please come home."

A few jerky paces, then stop, 20 breaths, a few more jerky paces. Like an automaton, the lonely figure continued in anguish and agony for hours. His lungs continued to fill. His breathing became more and more labored.

The ladder on The Second Step was horrible. Rung by frozen rung, he hung on for dear life as it swayed over the abyss. One step at a time, he told himself, one step at a time. Below, a brightly colored tent in Camp Six became his beacon.

Again and again he questioned whether he would make it to Camp Six. Again and again, he squeezed out his steps. Driven by his own weakening will and the love of his wife, daughters and the support of his teammates, painfully slowly, John retraced his steps toward The First Step.

Then, disaster. One of his crampons, those ice claws climbers attach to the bottom of their boots to grip the ice and snow, came off. He knew he would have to remove his mitts to re-attach it and if he did that, he could lose his fingers to frostbite.

Forced to make a decision between his fingers or his life, he set about the task of re-attaching the crampon. Fortunately, he had chemical hand-warmers in both mitts. They saved his fingers that day. When he stood up over half an hour later, he had a terrible shock. His chest felt unusually tight, like someone had wrapped a blood pressure bandage around his body and had pumped it up. He could now go no more than two or three steps before he had to stop and rest. Severe

> "John was in trouble. That's when I started getting worried. I began to get more fluids ready." — Dr. Denis Brown

pulmonary edema was taking hold.

"I started listening on the radio," Denis recalls. "... John was in trouble. That's when I started getting worried. I began to get more fluids ready."

When he got to the top of The First Step, John was horrified. Ahead of him was a 20-foot long section of knife-edge ridge no wider than 16 inches. On the way up, he had crossed it without even thinking. Now, cold, exhausted and dehydrated, it looked ghastly.

"I tried to walk across and I almost fell over down the face," he recalls.

Catching himself, he decided on a safer plan. Straddling it like a horse, he dragged himself to its end. Then, he slowly down-climbed The First Step. Camp 6 now looked deceptively close — like the summit had. He had to get there. He had to.

Then, what he feared more than anything — the dark.

"There was an amount of agitation that took place," he recalled. "... I did have a headlamp, but I didn't want to be out there by myself in the dark, totally exhausted. I just kept moving even though it seemed I was stopping more all the time. My rest stops were getting longer and longer. At first, I would take a five or 10-minute rest and only move another 50 or 60 feet and I'd stop and rest again. I could tell my body was really just shutting down... I really felt like sitting down and giving up."

John recalled all the organizational meetings we'd had as a team, ones in which we'd decided our primary goal was to come back alive. John didn't want to let the team down. Nor did he want to let Cathy-Anne, Leanne, or Alicia down either. He used their voices again to keep him going.

After what seemed like an eternity, John finally reached the point where he was to leave the northeast ridge and begin dropping down the north face toward camp. He stumbled and fell most of the way, grabbing and flailing at scattered pieces of rope. It seemed easier to slide than to stand.

Eventually, he reached a snow field about 200 feet long. That finished him.

"Getting across that was the hardest thing. It was almost knee deep. I ended up just crawling. I was totally thrashed and it was dark. But it was like, 'I am not going to give up now. I am so close.'"

Once, in desperation, he called out for Denis. But his words were whisked away by the wind. It didn't matter. Unknown to John, Denis was already on his way up to meet him.

"When I saw him, he was coming down very slowly," Denis recalls. "He was obviously in trouble because he would take a couple of steps, collapse, sit for a while and then try to move again."

When they met, not much was said. Although John was overjoyed, he was only able to moan. Together, the beleaguered pair made their way back to the tent.

Choosing People Over Peaks   14

It wasn't until they were both inside the tent at Camp Six that Denis realized the severity of the situation.

"John collapsed right back onto the wall of the tent," he recalls. "I thought, well, fine, let's get this guy lying down. I'll give him something to drink."

Immediately, John sat bolt upright. He grabbed Denis by his suit, clutching him like he was clutching life itself. His eyes telegraphed terror. His fingers squeezed so hard they went white.

"He started turning blue in front of me. He was frothing at the mouth and he couldn't breathe."

John was suffocating. By lying down, the liquid that had been building up in the bottom of his lungs spread instantly to his bronchial tubes, cutting off his air supply.

Locked in John's death-grip, there was no way Denis could grab the emergency oxygen tank he knew his patient desperately needed. So, with all the cool he could muster, he looked John straight in the eyes and calmly said:

"John, you have to calm down. Breathe slower. Breathe from the top of your lungs, right on top. You don't need that much oxygen. Take short, shallow breaths. You'll be okay."

It took some time for John's grip to loosen. When Denis

could free his hands, he quickly placed the oxygen mask on John's face.

"Just the way he talked to me was soothing," John recalls. "I recall the tone of his voice. I really felt okay... I didn't know what was happening to me. I thought, 'Here I fought all the way back and I am going to die right now. In the next three minutes, I am going to die.' Denis really reacted quickly... He didn't panic. I just recall his voice was peaceful. He wasn't upset or stressed or agitated. He knew exactly what was happening and I trusted him."

Within a minute, the crisis passed.

Over the next 45 minutes, John had three more attacks, but although they were frightening, none was as terrifying as the first. He knew he would come through them.

"It's not like I saw my daughters and now I am going to die," he said. "What is hidden inside our souls, and our minds, is first-most, survival."

Denis cranked the oxygen flow up to full. He began to administer powerful medications from his medical kit, but he knew John would have to descend. There is no cure for pulmonary edema except descent. Until his condition stabilized, however, that would be impossible.

We turned our backs on the summit and we went after our friend. Sometimes in life, there are more important things than getting to the goal.

Over the radio, we asked Denis to quantify on a scale of 1 to 10, the severity of John's condition — 1 being fine and 10 being death. Denis does not overstate things. He said, "Nine."

Thirty seconds later, we began preparations for a full-blown, high altitude rescue. We turned our backs on the summit and we went after our friend. Sometimes in life, there are more important things than getting to the goal. We looked for the larger picture. We found Jamie's galaxy.

First, we arranged for three Sherpas from another expedition to climb up to Camp Six at sunrise. Then, we sorted through our emergency oxygen at the North Col and prepared to send two men up the ridge after the Sherpas.

At about 2 a.m., John's oxygen tank began to empty. As John and Denis only had one bottle of emergency oxygen in Camp Six, Denis knew he would have to find another — soon.

"I felt right out on a limb," Denis recalls. "It was scary, even scarier than being in that hotel in Xegar with Jamie. I had no one to help me. I felt so alone."

In the tent next door was Australian Michael Rheinberger, himself preparing for his summit attempt. But none of the other climbers in Camp 6 knew what was happening. Because of the wind, it was useless to yell for help. Besides, they all had their own challenges to deal with.

With no option but to find more oxygen, Denis forced himself out of the tent and into the night. He pulled himself around to Michael's tent and woke him up. The Aussie was concerned.

"Are you sure you're okay?" he inquired.

"He was really good," Denis remembers. Michael explained that he hadn't any oxygen, but he thought he'd seen a bottle up by one of the higher tents in camp earlier in the day. So, Denis scrambled slowly up the slope.

Denis found the bottle of oxygen. He had no idea if it was full or empty. With one hand on a piece of anchored rope and one hand on the oxygen, he started to descend in the dark. There was just one problem — in his fatigue, he had not put his crampons on.

"I thought, 'If I drop this bottle, it's going straight down the mountain and if I slip, I'm going there too.' It was stupid, but I just didn't have the strength to find my crampons in the drifting snow."

If Denis had fallen, both John and he would have died. But Denis didn't fall. He had just enough energy left to get back to the tent.

"My rest in coming down early from my summit attempt was the key," he said later. "I had rested."

Denis crawled back into the tiny tent. As if by the grace of God, the tank fitting on the new bottle connected to John's mask. At the far end of the tent, John was propped up, sucking in the precious oxygen. At the door, Denis was squashed into one corner. He didn't sleep. He was too worried about John, and about his own right hand, which had become numb from carrying the freezing cold oxygen tank back to the tent. Together, on the edge of life, they waited for dawn.

At 10:30 a.m., the reinforcements arrived. In an amazing display of power, in five and a half hours, the three rescue Sherpas climbed a vertical distance of almost 3,000 feet without bottled oxygen, a super-human achievement at these altitudes. They arrived at John and Denis's tent like crampon-shod cavalry men, hauled John out and prepared to accompany the two weary climbers down the north ridge.

> If Denis had fallen, both John and he would have died. But Denis didn't fall. He had just enough energy left to get back to the tent.

"I was profoundly relieved," Denis recalls. "... We hugged. They were just great. They were fresh, strong, energetic, enthusiastic and confident. They just said, 'Let's go. We'll take you down.' They were wonderful, fantastic Sherpas.

"All I was thinking about now was saving John's life. We'd got through the night, by the skin of our teeth. I thought,

'Let's get a move on and get this guy down, because that's the only thing that will save him now.'"

John didn't want to move. He had exceeded himself mentally and physically in his summit attempt and all he wanted to do was stay in Camp Six. Thanks to Denis's soothing voice and manner, the oxygen and the medications he had received, a renewed warmth and stability had entered his life. It had become his rope to reality.

He knew, however, that there was another reality — death, if he didn't descend. So, stiff and groggy, barely aware mentally of what was going on, his body shifted into auto-pilot.

Using a Sherpa for support under each shoulder and with Denis behind holding him on a rope, they began to descend.

Below, in Camp Four, Mario and I had slapped on our emergency oxygen and headed up the ridge. We met the five men at about 25,000 feet.

When I came upon them, John was lying in the snow on his side. He hugged me. He could barely talk, but he could hear me. I gave him food and water.

"The brightness of those yellow expedition climbing suits really put on a smile," John recalls. "Then I started to feel sad that I hadn't made it to the top, now that I knew I was going to live, there was a guilt feeling. I really did try my best. Could I have done something different? I had failed."

"When I saw you (Alan) and Mario, I knew we were going to make it," Denis recalls. "We're going to be all right... It was fantastic. I remember being very, very confident when I met you guys. I knew we would get down."

It is ironic but true that in the mountains, just when you think you're safe, you can be in the greatest danger. On Everest especially, you cannot afford to let your guard down even for a second. While John's focus was shifting from survival to retrospection, we clipped him into the fixed rope and started to continue down the ridge. We had all our focus on John. Everything we had was directed toward saving his life.

We had forgotten about Denis. Denis had also made an attempt on the world's tallest peak without bottled oxygen and he had been up all night tending to his patient. He hadn't slept for at least four nights. Denis was also exhausted. A moment later, we found out exactly how exhausted he was.

To celebrate the moment and capture our joyous reunion, Denis stepped to one side to take a picture. Then, to my absolute horror, not more than 10 feet from me, Denis fell.

I can see him clearly now. He's sliding down the snow on his belly, spinning wildly out of control. His ice ax flies out of one hand. His camera flies out of the other. I hear him cry out, but there's nothing I can do.

It's obvious what's going to happen. He's going to follow the slope of the ridge off left and fall 4,000 feet to the Main Rongbuk Glacier.

Denis is going to die and there's nothing I can do but watch him fall.

It was like some kind of crazy, slow motion horror show. For some reason, I felt almost disconnected from the scene. I didn't feel any fear. I just defaulted to reporter mode. I picked up my radio and said: "Denis has fallen. Stand by for more information."

Denis stepped to one side to take a picture. Then, to my absolute horror, not more than 10 feet from me, Denis fell.

Then, a miracle happened. It had to be a miracle. It couldn't have been anything else.

There was a climber from another expedition coming up the ridge beneath us. In a split second, in the bravest display of mountaineering I have ever seen, that climber grabbed the fixed rope to which he was attached. He hauled it 15 feet to his left and got right under Denis. Just as Denis came down towards him, he football blocked Denis to a stop.

My stomach went into my mouth. I went down to the climber who had saved Denis's life, a climber whose name I didn't even know then, but whose name I'll certainly now never forget.

It was Constantine, a Romanian. We only know him by his first name, but we do know he saved Denis's life that day.

Mario and I went down to Constantine, we shook his hand, we gave him a great big hug and we said thank you for saving Denis's life.

In a split second, in the bravest display of mountaineering I have ever seen, that climber grabbed the fixed rope to which he was attached. He hauled it 15 feet to his left and got right under Denis. Just as Denis came down towards him, he football blocked Denis to a stop.

He looked back at us with this strangely calm look on his face and he said:

"I was meant to be here today."

Quickly, we dusted Denis off, clipped him into the rope and continued the descent. Denis seemed like he was in a state of shock and disbelief. He hardly said a word. I'm not sure he could really fathom what had just happened to him. None of us could. That didn't come until later.

"I don't know what happened," Denis recalls. "I stepped backwards and that was it... The next moment, I was spinning... and clutching desperately at the snow,

Choosing People Over Peaks

desperately trying to grab anything, trying to see if there was a hole, or a ledge or a rock, anything. But there was nothing.

"I knew I had fallen..., but I began to realize I couldn't stop myself. I don't know how to say this, but I just knew again I had lost control and that I was probably not going to make this one... I had the feeling this was it. This was the big one."

Even in his fatigue, John clearly remembers the scene.

"I felt, 'No! Don't let this happen because the man just saved my life.' It seemed so sad. It was almost like a bad movie or a bad book where the hero dies."

"As I spun around, I suddenly saw this person down below me," Denis recalls. "... It was almost like an awakening. Wow, I thought to myself. Here's a life grip that could possibly be just...

"When we made contact, I was ready for it... I clutched for dear life... I was ready to take hold of life again. I had given up a moment before.

"When I hit Constantine's legs, I clutched and pulled him off his feet. We both ended up hanging on the rope...

"I remember we just hung there. He was sort of kneeling in the snow and I was just hanging on to him. My head was still spinning and I kind of had to re-focus on reality."

The reality was clear: "I would have gone down into the main Rongbuk and that would have been the end of the story. If it hadn't been for that guy... "

Denis was sliding at about 15 miles an hour. He was wearing sharp crampons on the bottom of his boots. If Constantine had been hit by them anywhere on his body, it could have caused serious injury, even death. But he didn't even stop to think. He just reacted.

Constantine did not attain the summit that year. A year later, he did summit. It was like Everest had decided "Okay, you've earned the right." There is that sense about Everest, that she is watching and weighing from the world's highest bench. There is a higher code.

By now, the three Sherpa were far below us, descending at the same speed at which they had ascended — fast. Feeling the need to take charge, like a pair of drill sergeants, Mario and I literally marched John and Denis down toward Camp Four. As I barked out orders, the wind whipped clouds over the ridge making the whole scene seem surreal. I had tremendous clarity. We were on a mission.

When we finally reached Camp Four, it was a huge relief. There, we were met by Jamie and two doctors. Immediately, the physicians went to work on John.

The prognosis wasn't good.

— JAMIE —

After further medical examination, it was clear that if we didn't continue down, John would die. His condition had complicated into pneumonia as well as pulmonary edema and he was deteriorating by the minute.

Some 2,000 feet below, a make-shift hospital was being organized in Advance Base Camp. Between us and Advance Base Camp was that graveyard, the North Col slope.

John was no longer able to walk. He could barely talk. As I held him in my arms in one of the tents, I could hear his lungs were partially filled with liquid. Just breathing was choking him.

"I remember Jamie giving me some hot liquid," John says. "I remember feeling very warm and comfortable and at ease with myself and falling asleep. After that, the last thing I remember hearing was, 'Okay, John, we've got to move you.'"

"I didn't have any more energy to make decisions," Denis recalls. "John's pulse was horrible, he was ashen and he was gasping. I felt very shattered. That was the worst I'd felt. I realized then that, after all we'd done and come through, he might not make it."

John fell unconscious.

— ALAN —

Before the expedition, we had had long discussions about what to do if one team member's condition could potentially jeopardize the safety of the whole team. There we were, after all, on the top of the North Col slope. Night was falling. The temperature was dropping. Were we going to risk our lives by going into that graveyard in the dark? Would that be wise?

Before the expedition, in the calm and comfort of Canada, our decision had been unanimous. In such a situation, we all agreed that we would sacrifice the life of one team member to preserve the lives of the rest. It made sense.

But on the side of Everest, with John dying in Jamie's arms, the decision was easy. We threw the rule book out the tent door.

"Whatever it takes," Mario said stoically. "Whatever it takes to save John, we do it."

We sent Denis on ahead. If he was still able to stand when he got to Advance Base Camp, perhaps he could assist in readying the makeshift hospital there. Although he'd been up for days, he didn't even think about how exhausted he was. His patient's life was still in jeopardy. He knew he had to get intravenous drugs ready for John's arrival.

"Quickly, we attached a harness to John, put him in a

> *But on the side of Everest, with John dying in Jamie's arms, the decision was easy. We threw the rule book out the tent door.*

sleeping bag and loaded him into a rescue bag," Jamie recalls. "With a rope, we began lowering him 150 feet at a time down the slope. Mario went down with him to guide and I manned the anchor stations from above. From Advance Base Camp, Tim Rippel gave us directions over the radio."

Tim, of course, knew the slope well.

"I'm sure anybody who'd been lowered down that slope would have a definite feeling for it and a bonding sort of thought," Tim says. "It was a coincidental thing happening twice in the same place.

"I believe in fate and coincidences — what goes around, comes around."

— JAMIE —

I had never orchestrated a rescue like this before, nor was I formally trained in rescue procedures. But I have always found the logic of rope systems easy to grasp. With Tim's help, we set about the task. First, I lowered Mario and John together down the headwall of the North Col. As they disappeared outside the beam of my headlamp, I focused on the rope as it slid through my braking system. I was acutely aware that the lives of two people were literally running through my hands. I had no fear of dropping them though. I knew they were safe.

If I felt anything, it was anger. I was angry that we had come to climb a mountain and in the process might have killed our friend. Oddly, I also felt a tremendous sense of pride and happiness, and this caused some guilt. It was exhilarating to see the team working so well together for John. They were clearly forgetting themselves and working for the team. Unfortunately, a crisis had been needed to produce it. I wondered how such synergy could be created daily. Those moments were simultaneously the lowest and highest points of the expedition for me.

After I lowered them 150 feet, I would climb down to join them and unzip the bag John was in. I checked for his pulse and whispered in his ear, 'You'll be all right. We're almost down. Your girls are waiting for you.' He answered only with silence. Each time I did this, I remembered the words he had said to me in Camp Four before he fell unconscious: 'Don't let me die, Jamie. Don't let me die.'

Then, I'd zip up the bag and watch him disappear into the dark hole of the night. A part of me didn't want to let him go. I wasn't sure if he'd still be alive when I next saw him.

> I also felt a tremendous sense of pride and happiness, and this caused some guilt. It was exhilarating to see the team working so well together for John. They were clearly forgetting themselves and working for the team. Unfortunately, a crisis had been needed to produce it.

— ALAN —

As if providentially, the wind died. A clear, but cold moon rose over Everest. It bathed the North Col slope in eerie light, illuminating our way down. There was a strange sense to the scene. It was like the eye of a hurricane. Was it coincidence?

Jamie radioed out to the other expeditions for help. There were nine other teams climbing Everest at the time. He asked those climbers who were available to come out. If we got John down the slope to the glacier below, he knew we'd need help. Some of us had been awake for several days, hadn't eaten anything and had had little to drink — a recipe for disaster.

At one point during the lowering of John, the rope jammed. Mario had to rectify the situation by physically pulling John back up the slope for four or five feet. At 22,000 feet, by himself, this required a super-human effort. Only a man with the size and strength of Mario could have done it.

They were sacrificing their own energy and summit chances to rescue someone in the middle of the night, someone who wasn't even from their own country or team.

"I had to pull, climb, carry John," Mario remembers. "It took all the strength I had left. I was almost screaming. 'Shit Bilodeau! Pull man! Pull!'"

He did. We all did in our own way when it was required. For those hours of trial, we were more closely united than at any other time on the expedition, perhaps at any time in our lives.

Just as John was disappearing over the edge of a block of ice, Jamie looked down to the glacier below. He saw a snake of lights winding its way up towards the bottom of the slope. At first, he was perplexed. Then he realized it was the headlamps of other climbers coming to help John. They were sacrificing their own energy and summit chances to rescue someone in the middle of the night, someone who wasn't even from their own country or team.

Mario saw the lights too.

"At that point, I knew John was safe," he recalls. "It was the most emotional time for me on the expedition. I felt the strength of the power of the people on the mountain, the people that just said, 'Well, we have a mountain to climb, but first we have a person to save.' Everyone all joined together."

That's part of the reason we climb Everest. We climb for

the shared struggle, for the togetherness and for each other. We start at the bottom of the mountain as a loosely assembled group of individuals, each from our own country with our own egotistical goals. But we finish as one — one equal temper of hearts working together to survive.

At 12:30 a.m. on May 27, two days after John and Denis had begun their summit bid, we all arrived safely at the base of the North Col slope. We were greeted by a welcoming party of climbers toting vacuum flasks of tea and hot chocolate, cookies and extra clothes. Lhakpa Sonam took my pack and gave me a big hug. "It's okay, Alan," he said warmly. "We take over. We take over."

I was almost moved to tears. It was like a homecoming, a feeling of sanctuary and support. I have never felt more cared for. Somewhere on that big, cold, lonely mountain, someone cared.

We start at the bottom of the mountain as a loosely assembled group of individuals, each from our own country with our own egotistical goals. But we finish as one — one equal temper of hearts working together to survive.

As each member of our team was paired with a support climber, John was loaded onto a rescue litter and pulled carefully down the glacier to the moraine. There, he was carried for short distances at a time, placed gently on the ground while the team rested, then lifted and carried forward a short distance again.

I was last off the slope that night. I remember watching the small army of rescuers and thinking, "This is unbelievable. Is this really happening?" It was — and it continued to happen. As the troop disappeared off into the moonlight, for an hour I kept hearing their inspirational rallying cry:

"One, two, three — lift!"

Finally, at 1:30 a.m., we returned safely to Advance Base Camp. There, Sally's kitchen tent had been converted into an emergency room. Inside, a team of three physicians, including Denis and two others who had met us on the Col, attended to John. They hooked up intravenous fluids, antibiotics and steroids, gave him fresh oxygen and shot him full of emergency medications. Sally quietly oversaw the whole drama with concern and sensitivity.

I remember saying goodnight to John that night. I said good-bye to him too. I felt there was a good chance I would never see him alive again. His eyes flickered open and closed involuntarily. I couldn't know if his finger twitches were the last signs of life or not. His face was deathly pale and his oxygen mask dripped with condensation from his shallow breathing. Wrapped in sleeping bags and with tubes going into him every which way, he looked more like a mummy than a mountaineer. At any moment, I thought his spirit might rise up in the moonlight, follow me out of the tent and turn toward the top again.

"When we got John back to Advance Base Camp, I was happier than any summit could have made me," Jamie says. "My near-death experience in that hotel in Xegar gave me a new appreciation for life. That appreciation was heightened by John's effort to stay alive."

At 2:30 a.m., Dr. Stuart Hutchison, of Montreal, ushered us away. Denis didn't want to go. He wanted to sleep by John and safeguard him through the night. Stuart would not hear of it. If John was still alive at 7 a.m., he explained, we might still have to carry him the 13 miles to Base Camp.

"Get some rest," he said. "You may need it in a few hours."

By now, the rescue had been going for 33 hours. We

were all exhausted, but none of us slept. We were too afraid.

Stuart watched over John for the next four and a half hours. At 7:30 a.m., I rolled out of my tent and went to the kitchen tent where John was housed. I stood outside the door for a moment trying to get up the courage to open it. I was afraid to look inside. I didn't want to see him dead. I didn't want to know that all our effort had been in vain. Finally, I willed myself to reach for the door handle. Tentatively, I pulled the latch, swung the door open and I stepped inside.

I looked straight into John's face. His eyes stared blankly back at me and for a split second, my heart fell. I searched for a sign of life.

There wasn't one. No, wait, his right index finger seemed to be moving. Was it? I looked more closely. Yes. Yes. It was moving. But was he doing it or was it just his body?

I looked back at his face. His dark eyes seemed to narrow. His lips looked like they were moving.

His eyes stared blankly back at me and for a split second, my heart fell. I searched for a sign of life. There wasn't one. No, wait, his right index finger seemed to be moving.

My heart skipped a beat. John wasn't dead. John was alive! He was alive and breathing and motioning for me to come forward. I sprang to his side and put my ear to his lips.

"Hobson," he said in the feeblest of voices. "... You need a shave."

I hugged him. I wanted to squeeze him so hard it might have really killed him, but I just gave him a gentle squeeze. With my touch, I tried to communicate beyond words how happy I was. Then I knelt beside him and looked again into his eyes. He looked back at me as if to say: "Nice to see you, buddy. It's been a while."

It was a great moment. It stays with me to this day. I can still see his face, and those raccoon eyes staring back at me. He'd survived. He was still among us.

Then I knelt beside him and looked again into his eyes. He looked back at me as if to say: "Nice to see you, buddy. It's been a while."

"When I came to, Sally was stroking my head," John remembers. "She was talking in a very calm sort of way, telling me where I was and explaining what had happened. 'You're okay,' she said quietly. 'You're okay.'"

Denis was there too.

"Thanks for being there, Alan," he said. "Promise me you won't give up. I love you."

On the morning of May 28, just a day after we got him to Advance Base Camp, John sat up. That afternoon, he walked. Four days after that, with the help of Da Nuru Sherpa, John McIsaac, a man who without doubt had a foot in the grave and then some, walked under his own steam back to Base Camp. En route, he walked into the arms of his wife, Cathy-Anne.

Today, John has totally recovered. His heart and lungs have returned to normal and he has suffered no ill effects whatsoever from his Everest experience. In fact, he continues to adventure and climb the world over and of course, to spend time with his girls.

The Power of Passion

Refusing to Fold 15

Some climbers were not as fortunate as John. Michael Rheinberger, the Australian who told Denis where he could find more oxygen for John, made his seventh attempt on Everest as John was recovering in Advance Base Camp. Michael made it to the summit, but ran out of oxygen on the descent and died.

He wasn't the only one. A Taiwanese climber called Norman, left Camp Six too late on the morning of his summit attempt and refused to listen to his Sherpa's pleadings not to continue.

"I don't descend, I only go up," one of his Sherpas said Norman had told him. "How can I go back to 20 million other Taiwanese a disgrace?"

Norman continued solo to the summit, but because of cloud and high wind conditions on top, became disoriented and went down the wrong side of the mountain. By the time he realized his error, it was too late. After struggling for more than a day to get back on track, he finally collapsed in the snow on the summit pyramid. He may well sit there still.

Stone memorials were erected for Michael and Norman near Base Camp.

"For us, it was a powerful reminder that sometimes it

takes more courage and strength to turn your back on a goal than to continue," Jamie says. "One of those stones could have easily read: 'John McIsaac.'"

For us, the deaths of Michael and Norman raised larger questions about the meaning of success. John had missed the summit by a little over 500 vertical feet, but returned alive. Michael Rheinberger and Norman had made it to the top, but perished on the descent.

As our team wrestled with these and other deeply personal issues, we began to contemplate a second summit attempt.

We didn't have to contemplate long. We had no equipment left. It had either been lost in the avalanche on the north face or used trying to put John and Denis on top. We had no emergency oxygen left. We had used all of it rescuing John. In fact, we had purchased oxygen from other teams during John's rescue.

Finally, we were spent physically and emotionally. We had given everything we had saving John. We were shells of men now with little left inside us. The bright light of our ambition had been extinguished.

"I remember walking to the outhouse the morning after John's rescue," Mario says. "I had to stop three times in 30 feet. When I got there, I just sat on a rock and I couldn't move anymore. I was exhausted — completely finished, gone. I had no more strength. All the strength we had left, we'd used."

Sometimes it takes more courage and strength to turn your back on a goal than to continue.

Realizing for the second time that we would not make it to the summit, we turned our backs on Everest. As we descended, we cleaned up the mountain, leaving it cleaner than when we had arrived. We called forth our yaks and yak herders to help carry our gear down the mountain, and slowly, we descended to Base Camp.

Not much was said. There was not much to say. We had given it everything we had. For a second time, we had not made it to the top. We knew some would say we had failed.

My twin brother, James, in Ottawa, was not one of them. He dispatched a message to the team in Base Camp:

"This expedition has been a tremendous display of heart, soul and perseverance, quite an uplifting experience for all of us back in Canada. The victory truly lies in the effort and all of you have pushed yourselves to the limit. Hope you can hear our cheering and applause from halfway around the world — despite the howling winds around you."

My parents sent similar sentiments:

"Congratulations to you and the Canadian team on Mount Everest this May! You have sustained yourselves on 'the edge of human performance' in its broadest sense... Let us say from here that you have all demonstrated attributes that elevate the human condition and so are an inspiration to us all. May love abide with you — winners all."

One of the most touching dispatches came from Fred Balm. He wrote:

"Sometimes hard decisions need to be made with the set goal close at hand. It is during moments like these when human beings show their true courage to let wisdom prevail over aspiration.

"You have set an example of determination incomprehensible to those observing from down here... You are being closely followed by a larger number of Canadian supporters than I ever thought possible."

— JAMIE —

I felt little disappointment about not reaching the top and I still feel that way today. The team was more important to me than the goal itself and unfortunately, throughout the stress of the expedition, my relationship with some of the team members deteriorated. I assume some responsibility for this and unfortunately, the fact that some of these relationships did not continue after the climb has been far more disappointing to me than not reaching the summit.

"So often we measure ourselves by a start and finish and we say that if we don't quite finish something, we have failed in life," John McIsaac recalls. "I have learned a lot about myself from that incident (the rescue)... I learned that I am a human being and I have weaknesses and strengths and I have learned to live with them. It (the summit bid) really put me in my place. Until that time, I thought there was no problem. I am going to stand on top... I really felt shattered when I didn't get that success... What we did on Everest in '94 really opened up my eyes... I realized I'm not going to be able to do everything I think I can do, so I must go about my life doing the best I can and waking up every day knowing that I am doing that."

In Base Camp, someone dug through our boxes and pulled out two bottles of champagne. At first, we didn't think that would be enough for a party. But after two and a half months on Everest, 14 tired people who have all lost weight can have a heck of a good party on two bottles of champagne.

> *Alan and I have learned some pretty powerful lessons. Everest has changed our lives, changed the way we think and act, the way we live.*

Then, it hit us. It wasn't the champagne. Nor was it a rationalization. Our spirits began to soar when we started to savor the satisfaction of having saved John's life, of being together in Base Camp laughing and joking as a team. A satisfaction came over Alan and me far more meaningful than either of us had felt on any summit.

In our two expeditions to Everest, Alan and I have learned some pretty powerful lessons. Everest has changed our lives, changed the way we think and act, the way we live. We have learned that when we set ourselves lofty goals in life, goals we all have regardless of what mountain or mountains we're climbing, we're going to mess up sometimes. We're going to be hit by some avalanches. We may even fall into the odd crevasse. There will be setbacks. And yes, there will be failures.

It's okay to fail.
It's not okay
to fold.

— ALAN —

Jamie and I have learned that it's okay to fail. Failure is part of the success process. We cannot have success without failure. They go hand in hand.

It's okay to fail. It's not okay to fold.

Jamie and I have no intention of folding. As we said at the beginning of our story, we're going back to Everest. By the time you read this, the Colliers/Lotus Notes Everest Expedition will be history.

In keeping with our philosophy of continuous improvement, we've made a few changes this time.

First, we'll be attempting Everest from the southern, Nepalese side of the mountain. The route we have chosen, the South Col (the one climbed by Sir Edmund Hillary, Sherpa Tenzing Norgay and the British team in 1953) is about half the length of the routes we have attempted on the north side. We first went to the north side in 1991 because we were part of a team that had a permit on the north side. We went back there in 1994 because we were familiar with it. With two expeditions to the north side behind us, we believe we have a greater chance of summiting on the south side. The route is shorter and steeper. In high altitude climbing, you want to get up and down as quickly as possible.

Second, we have hired a professional expedition organizer, Steve Matous, of Boulder, Colorado, whom we met on Everest in 1994. As we learned the hard way last time, we cannot hope to fund-raise for an expedition, organize it, lead it and then climb the mountain. There is only enough energy for one task. This time, we will be climbers.

Third, we have raised more money, but reduced the size of our North American climbing team. More money means less energy and time needed approaching companies to supply products or services. If we need a dozen sleeping bags, we buy them. It's simpler.

Fourth, our team is to consist of several specialty teams: a fund-raising team, an organizing team, a support team, a route-fixing team, and a summit team.

Finally, our expedition will be bringing oxygen. If, on summit day, we are feeling healthy, the wind is calm, the snow is hard and the temperature is warmer than usual, we may make an attempt without bottled oxygen.

In spite of our disagreements, our differences in character, methods of operation, priorities, personalities and opinions, we have so far been able to keep our friendship together.

Jamie and I climb for the shared struggle, to be with others, with each other and alone with ourselves. We climb up, we fall back, we climb up again. We fight. We disagree. We reconcile. In spite of our disagreements, our differences in character, methods of operation, priorities, personalities and opinions, we have so far been able to keep our friendship together. We hope to continue. We share a mutual respect for each other and a commitment toward common goals.

Regardless of whether we make it to the top in 1997 or not, my goal is to have positive closure with Everest. I want to arrive in Base Camp on an equal playing field with the other people who come to Everest — not as a burned out fund-raiser, organizer and communications coordinator, but as a fit, healthy, and well-rested climber.

Jamie says he feels much the same way: "The months of organizational stress in 1994 left me weak. I wonder if perhaps I just didn't have what was needed. In 1997, I plan to find out if that was the case or not."

Whatever the outcome of the 1997 expedition, I want to know I gave it everything I had, short of my life. That way, there will be no dishonor. When the expedition is over, my goal is to turn the page and begin a new chapter of my life. After Everest, I'm going to re-marry, learn to fly a helicopter, ride my mountain bike more, drink plenty of milkshakes and buy a dog — a golden Labrador or a Cocker Spaniel. I'd like to get off the hill for a while and enjoy the flats. For 39 years, achievement has been my primary focus of life. I would now like to focus on enjoyment. Achievement has its rewards and it can be enjoyable, but I have found it lonely. Training and writing are solitary activities. So is public speaking. You fly to a strange city, book into a hotel room, stand up in front of a group of people you have never met, speak and then fly to the next city. There is little opportunity to develop any lasting relationships because you are never in one place long enough to form any.

After Everest, I choose not to focus my life on Everest anymore. I am tired of training and fund raising. Going to Everest three times is like preparing for three successive Olympic Games, except that in our case, Jamie and I have chosen to raise the finances and organize the Games as well as participate in them.

Of late, the label of "Alan Hobson, Everest Adventurer" has begun to wear a little thin. There is more to me than an adventurer. In a bizarre twist, I like the attention Everest brings, but I dislike the narrowness of the image I have created for myself. I long to be known and loved for more than just being "The Everest Guy." There's nothing "Mountain Man" about me really. I get cold easily, I would rather sleep in a bed than a sleeping bag any day, and I dislike eating food out of plastic bags with my hands for more than a few days at a time — something we do for weeks on Everest. I put up with it because it is part of the price we pay to climb the mountain.

Some days, I'd just like to wake up and be "normal". But I am driven. Something sends me out the door to far off places, in search of something that's probably inside me, if I could just stop long enough to find it. I keep hearing this clock ticking in my head that says, "hurry, hurry" and I've spent most of my life racing it. I believe I cannot escape my restlessness anymore than a leopard can change its spots. Perhaps I can change. Perhaps I cannot.

In a naive way, I hope I will have more personal peace if I make it safely to and from the summit. I will have succeeded in doing the most difficult physical thing I could imagine. This will be a source of tremendous personal satisfaction and pride.

And what if I don't make it? It will be deeply disappointing, but I have many new goals to live for. At this point in my life, I keep climbing because I must. I must see how high I can climb. I must know the answer. I must have peace with myself.

— JAMIE —

My time in the mountains has changed my perspective

on success. The change started with my journey to Everest in 1991 and came to fruition with the 1994 climb. Before 1991, success meant the relentless pursuit of an end by various means. I would train, arrange logistics and raise funds to achieve the desired end on Everest — the summit. This process makes sense when we look at means and ends in a traditional linear sense, that is, all means should lead consecutively to desired ends. But I have come to understand, through my adventuring, that for me, this notion of success is

Everest became an intense reason to attack each day and better myself in numerous ways. ...Each day and often each hour, I realize a goal and enjoy the satisfaction of being my best in the process.

upside down. In fact, a traditional end — the summit, an Olympic gold medal, or wealth — only serves as a navigational tool, a marker to give the process direction. The end for me is a greater depth and breadth of character. I measure this in terms of greater integrity, better business and communication skills and a higher personal motivation to train and become stronger. More simply, my end is to become as internally knowledgeable and as externally aware as possible. The process, the experience, the struggle, the hard-won lessons, these are ends in themselves. Everest became an intense reason to attack each day and better myself in numerous ways. My end has become the traditional means. Each day and often each hour, I realize a goal and enjoy the satisfaction of being my best in the process.

This change in perspective has been powerfully liberating for me. I am able to extract greater enjoyment from each day. With daily reward and fulfillment, I no longer look solely to the future for my happiness. I have it now, and this immediacy gives me contentment. From this contentment I derive peace. After the Everest climb in 1997, I will continue to adventure in the mountains as I always have.

— ALAN —

In 1991, Jamie and I went to Everest as part of a $1 million expedition. The team consisted of 20 expedition members and tens of thousands of dollars in bottled oxygen. With all those resources, we finished some 3,500 vertical feet short of the top, at 25,500 feet.

"Our business in life is not to get ahead of others, but to get ahead of ourselves, to break our own records, to outstrip our yesterday by our today, to do our work with more force than ever before." — Stewart B. Johnson

Jamie and I went back three years later with half the budget, half the personnel and no bottled oxygen. Our team finished triumphantly at 28,500 feet, just 500 vertical feet shy of the summit — a quantum leap forward at these altitudes. That quantum leap was made possible because we sat down and looked at what other people had called "a failure" and turned it into a success. Many people still ask us, "Why are you two going back a third time? What more is there to learn? What further progress can possibly be made beyond the roughly 500 vertical feet your team left behind the last time?"

We think the answer is best

summarized in the words of Stewart B. Johnson. He said:

"Our business in life is not to get ahead of others, but to get ahead of ourselves, to break our own records, to outstrip our yesterday by our today, to do our work with more force than ever before."

In the weeks and months and years ahead, we all have the opportunity to live by this adage, whether we're trying to be better climbers, better business people, better parents, better partners, or just better friends.

> *Jamie and I believe success is coming home to someone who loves us.... It's knowing we're not alone, feeling we belong and knowing that somehow, somewhere, someone cares.*

Jamie and I have been endeavoring to apply Johnson's philosophy in our friendship. This book is an example. At the time this book was written, Jamie was working full out on the '97 expedition. While he focused on working with our expedition leader/organizer, sponsors and suppliers, I focused on writing this book. We intend to continue to use the strength of our partnership to achieve multiple goals simultaneously, to in effect "do our work with more force than ever before." We will both share in the success of this book, just as we will share in the success of the expedition.

But what is success? Is it what advertising tells us it is? Is it owning that car, or boat, or home? Or is it the journey Jamie talks about?

What's truly meaningful to all of us as human beings really has very little to do with how high we climb on our mountains. That is important, but it is not "all important".

Jamie and I believe success is coming home to someone who loves us. It's a smile from our partner or the caring shoulder of a friend. It's knowing we're not alone, feeling we belong and knowing that somehow, somewhere, someone cares. Amid the chaos of change around us, there is someone waiting for us at the bottom of the slope.

People can help provide us with that sanctuary, provided we are first at peace with ourselves. People make our planet what it is. People are more precious than peaks.

"I really love being on an expedition," says Mario. "I really love being in a group of people intensively active and intensively in contact with nature and all the exchange of emotion we live through together. The beauty of an expedition isn't only being on the mountain. It's being on the mountain with people and sharing with people."

"We share our lives with each other (on an expedition)," Tim says. "We pretty much know everything there is to know about each other, past and hopefully, present. Mountains are beautiful things to do and if you can get up on them, by all means, get up on them. But if you don't summit, you still had the good times, you still have the good feelings and you come out of it alive and looking to do other things with those people or with other people."

It was relationships that made our experiences on Everest what they were. Constantine and Denis were somehow linked when he fell. So were Mario and Lhakpa on the north face; Tim and Jamie during John's rescue; Dil, Ram, Zit, Jamie and I during the mudslides; our team and the rest of the teams at the base of the North Col slope; and John and his girls on his descent. Even Tim had a strange connection with that yak that took him to Base Camp in '91.

In retrospect, so much of our Everest experiences have been about interconnectedness — Fred Balm and me for sponsorship; Jamie and Mike Keller for Jamie's background; Denis and Jamie during his near-death experience in Xegar; even Constantine and Everest. It was like a domino effect sparked by commitment — or by something else.

At one time I didn't believe in coincidence. I used to

think that we created our own coincidences, like our own "luck." We attracted that which occurred solely through our actions. After two Everest expeditions, I'm not so sure. Even a scientist like my father would have a hard time discounting the examples above.

And, there are more. Jamie and Susan could have died on the Tibetan plateau. John and Denis could have died on the ridge. Mario and Lhakpa could have died on the north face. None of them did. Was it just good fortune?

Perhaps there was a reason Tim injured his knee in '91 — to help us gain rescue experience on the North Col slope that would help save John's life in '94.

And perhaps Denis's summit bid had to end early so he would have enough energy left to save his partner. Maybe Constantine's role wasn't to make it to the top in '94, but in fulfilling the preordained, he earned the right to stand on top a year later. Maybe I was supposed to be asked to write Fred Balm's profile, to help put a communications system together so Jamie and I could connect John with his daughters half a world away precisely when he most needed to hear their voices.

What enabled Jamie to connect the radios to the satellite telephone and pull off that press conference in '91 with seconds to spare? Was it just a technological fluke? What was that presence that told John it was time to turn around at his high point in '94? Was it only intuition borne from experience, or was it something else? Maybe Mario wasn't supposed to die on the north face because he would be needed to help save John. Why did the moon rise exactly when we needed it to light our way to the bottom of the North Col slope?

Is there a power associated with Everest? Is there a higher power predetermining all these things? Is there a higher power, period?

I don't pretend to know. What I can say is that the

people who share this planet and the events of our lives are more closely linked than any of us may know. Our world extends far beyond the boundaries of our senses, and, indeed, extends well beyond the summit of Everest. We are climbers connected by an invisible rope. We struggle up similar mountains, sometimes a world apart, but only a few relationships away.

For me, there is no finer example of connected coincidence than John McIsaac and Michael Hobson, two apparently unrelated individuals linked through me. By the time of John's rescue, Michael Hobson's body had begun to make its own new healthy bone marrow and the little boy was well on his way to a full recovery. Doctors estimated he had a one in 20,000 chance of finding a donor match. Today, Michael enjoys almost perfect health.

The bone marrow donor, I was to find out later, was Jeff Krueger, 31, of Calgary, a man who worked for a sponsor of our 1991 climb.

That sponsor was recruited by John McIsaac.

Jamie and I recall the words of Scottish mountaineer, W. (Bill) H. Murray:

> *The people who share this planet and the events of our lives are more closely linked than any of us may know.... We are climbers connected by an invisible rope.*

"Until you are committed there is hesitancy, the chance to draw back, ineffectiveness. There is one elementary truth about all acts of initiative and creativity, the ignorance of which kills countless ideas and splendid plans: the moment one definitely commits oneself, then Providence moves. All sorts of things begin to happen to help you that would never otherwise have occurred. A whole stream of events issues from that decision, raising in your favor all manner of unforeseen incidents, meetings and material assistance, which you couldn't have dreamt would come your way.

"I have learned a deep respect for one of Goethe's couplets, which bears repeating:

"'Are you in earnest? Seize this very minute. What you can do, or dream you can, begin it. Boldness has genius, power and magic in it.'"

— JAMIE —

Our two expeditions increased my appreciation of two things: the importance of individuals over ambitions and my spiritual connection to the mountains.

For three years, our whole focus had been to make it to the top. We had done everything to get there. No sacrifice had been too great.

On Everest, we were forced to make a choice between the summit and John's life, between a peak and a person. We chose the person.

It wasn't until we got to Base Camp that we realized the powerful result of that decision. When we looked at the memorials for Michael and Norman, then around at each other, we knew we had succeeded. We had certainly succeeded in saving a life. Summits may come and go, summit photographs may fade, but the satisfaction of saving John will stay with us forever.

The time I spend in the mountains has become my link between myself and others like John, my family and friends. It has also become the link between the self I find in personal exploration and the self that lies beyond me. My sense of connectedness is a web of being. The dramatic times when our connectedness taps us on the shoulder or smacks us square in the face produce a great sense of awe, but they are really just moments when the strands of the web are plucked by fate and happenstance. They remind us we are part of the greater whole, that there is a wisdom beyond ourselves. It can play these strands of our lives like a symphony — sometimes discordant and jarringly, but more often, harmonious and full of beauty. This connected exploration is why I will continue to climb and adventure for years to come.

— ALAN —

Jamie and I are connected in a way that, like Everest, continues to change. After the '94 expedition and the resulting fall out in our friendship, we have worked hard to try to rebuild our relationship. We have been to counseling and have talked through our respective positions regarding leadership and goals during that trip. It has not been easy and we are still a long way from where we want to be, but we remain committed to making things work in our partnership and friendship. All this discussion has created greater clarity in our goals for our next expedition and for our friendship. We have learned from our past. Our priorities are clear: first, come back alive; second, come back friends; and third, come back with the summit.

Health and weather permitting, Jamie and I hope to be the first summit team. Someone else is leading. We are climbing.

Our dream is to stand on the summit together, to look at each other with the world at our feet, think about that day on the moraine in Advance Base Camp in '91, smile and say proudly, "Thanks to you my friend, WE DID IT!"

> *No matter how steep the slope,*
> *No matter how severe the cold,*
> *We can tie a knot and hang on,*
> *But we must always keep climbing.*
>
> *— A Climber's Rule*

They Did It!!!

On May 23, 1997, Alan and Jamie realized their dream! At 7 a.m., under a perfect blue sky and light winds, Jamie stretched his arms toward the heavens and slowly turned around 360° on the top of Everest. Two hours later, Alan also reached the summit of Mount Everest. "If there is a lesson in all of this," Alan said from the summit as his voice cracked with emotion, "it is that if we persevere long enough, we can do the dreams."

Read All About It

You can read the whole inspirational story of this third expedition to Everest in their next book to be released in the fall of 1998!

The Power of Passion

About the Authors

Alan Hobson and Jamie Clarke are two of North America's most dynamic adventurers and speakers. Together, they have trademarked their own business niche as "Adventrepreneurs"™ — adventurers and entrepreneurs.

In 1991, Alan and Jamie put the first live Canadian telephone reports off Mount Everest via satellite, an effort for which they were nominated for the Order of Canada, the highest honor that can be bestowed on Canadian civilians.

Since then, they have gone on to co-organize the 1994 Emergo Mount Everest Expedition. Its goal was to put the first Canadians on the top of Everest without the use of bottled oxygen. In 1997, they returned to Everest as the founders of the Colliers/Lotus Notes Everest Expedition.

But they are far from just climbers. Jamie is a former triple Canadian junior cross-country ski champion, a broadcaster and an award-winning public speaker. Alan is a former nine-time "All-American" gymnast (even though he is a Canadian), the author of five books on adventure and achievement and the winner of the William Randolph Hearst Award for Excellence in News Writing. They have adventured from Everest to the Andes and from the Arctic to Africa.

Each year, Alan and Jamie speak to hundreds of corporate and public audiences worldwide. Their client list includes the likes of General Motors, J.P. Morgan, Dean Witter, Johnson & Johnson and Merrill Lynch. Audiences are consistently thrilled by their presentations and riveted by their messages. Alan and Jamie believe everyone is climbing their own Everests.

There's More

To order more copies of *The Power of Passion*, to order a copy of the documentary *Above All Else*, their 1997 summit video and to book Alan or Jamie for a speaking presentation, contact:

Jamie Clarke	**Alan Hobson**
tel: (403) 230-2760	tel: (403) 262-1806
fax: (403) 230-2773	fax: (403) 262-6326
email: karebear@jamieclarke.com	email: iei@cadvision.com
www.jamieclarke.com	
www.alwaysadventure.net	

The Power of Passion